KATHARINE ASQUITH'S NURSING DIARY

Katharine Asquith's Nursing Diary

St Omer 16th April—24th August 1918
VAD nurse

Introduced and edited by

John Jolliffe

&

Raymond Oxford

Anthony Eyre

MOUNT ORLEANS PRESS

Published in a limited edition
of 200 copies by
Anthony Eyre, Mount Orleans Press,
Cricklade, Wiltshire
in April 2025

© Mells Estate Archive 2025
All rights reserved
Unless otherwise indicated illustrations
are from the Mells Estate Archive

ISBN 9781912945511

A CIP record for this book can be
obtained from the British Library

Typeset in 11/15pt Joanna Nova

Printed in India by
Imprint Press

Contents

Introduction   7

St Omer   15

Appendix: The Haunted House   71

A family group, before the War: Katharine (seated, fifth from left) looks up at Raymond.

Introduction

IN APRIL 1918, Katharine Asquith, née Horner, was aged 33, married since 1907 to Raymond, the eldest son of the Prime Minister, H.H. Asquith, and mother of three children then aged nine, seven and two. Raymond had been killed in 1916 on the Somme and her only surviving brother, Edward Horner, in 1917. Her life had been shattered and she has been described as one of the most tragic of all the war widows.

Her intellectual interests were advanced. While a nurse, she would read Tolstoy's *Resurrection*, Pascal's *Lettres Provinciales*, Bosanquet's *Suggestions on Ethics* and on a lighter note Lytton Strachey's *Eminent Victorians*, which she enjoyed. Stimulated by Raymond's fluency in ancient Latin and Greek, she had earlier taught herself to read Greek literature in the original. She loved Shakespeare's plays, with a special place for *Hamlet*. She wrote short pieces of poetry (see pp. 57-8 & 69) and later benefited greatly from literary friendships with Belloc and Maurice Baring, who played a part in her joining the Catholic Church in 1923, as well as (at a later stage) with Evelyn Waugh and Siegfried Sassoon who were frequent visitors at her home at Mells, in east Somerset. She was a shrewd literary critic, e.g. in her comments on *Bérénice* by Racine and on James Joyce.

She was also one of an emancipated group of friends who, long before the War, came to be nicknamed by the unsympathetic as the 'Corrupt Coterie'. Though personally loyal to their parents, the so-called 'Souls', they were openly indifferent to the social conventions and standards of the older generation. They delighted in Nijinsky and Bakst but had yet to adopt the Cubists and Picasso. Their antinomian, comfortable way of life was sharply interrupted

Katharine in pre-War years.

when war came, and they immediately accepted the strict disciplines required of those like Katharine and her great friend, Diana Manners, who became nurses. Practical domestic details had previously not been their strong point. In an early letter to Frances Horner, thanking her for a visit to Mells when Katharine had been left in charge of catering, Raymond had reported that 'We had Aunt's Leg [a rather heavy and primitive kind of pudding] for lunch twice, and would have had it again if Katharine had remembered to order it.' Heavy drinking was acceptable now and then and the consumption of morphia, codenamed 'Muffy', was not unknown. Many details of their activities can be found in such books as *The Children of the Souls* by Jeanne MacKenzie.

Katharine's marriage had been far closer and richer than most, and in her despair when it was over she joined one of a number of private hospitals set up in France and Egypt by rich ladies determined to do what they could, closer to the front lines than most of the British military hospitals, to care for the stream of casualties that were being suffered on active service, including many of their own

Above and below: before the move to the huts: the Duchess of Sutherland's Hospital in more prestigious surroundings.

Millie Sutherland portrayed by Victor Tardieu, inscribed: À Madame la duchesse M. de Sutherland: Hommage respectueux et très reconnaissant d'un simple soldat — Victor Tardieu, Bourbourg Avril 1915
(Florence Nightingale Museum)

families and friends. One of the very first, which Katharine was to join, was that set up by Millicent Duchess of Sutherland, then aged 48 and herself recently widowed and (unhappily) remarried in haste. Millie's organisational ability and experience, together with her exalted social position and wide range of contacts, including some in Germany (where she had even met the Kaiser), her tact and patience in the face of endless obstacles, all combined to make it a notable success. She was to act as General Manager and Matron throughout the war, though she chose to be addressed by all as Sister Millicent.

As the Germans advanced the hospital had to be moved twice, and by April 1918 it was based in St Omer, near Boulogne, as an Advanced Dressing Station, then designated a Casualty Clearing Station: here the wounded were cared for before being moved to full scale hospitals. It consisted of seven makeshift wards, in huts built appropriately by German prisoners. From Namur to St Omer, by the end of the war it had cared for 8,000 patients, of whom 6,000 were British, the rest being French, Belgians, Americans and the occasional German. A detailed account of it may be found in chapter 10 of Millicent's biography, Dear Duchess, by Denis Stuart (1982). Two brief quotations add to the picture. Hugh MacCorquodale, a badly wounded officer married to the popular novelist Barbara Cartland, wrote to her that Millie 'looked like an angel. She came round, looking so beautiful, that men who were actually dying revived because she gave them hope... something they longed for. She was like a dream to those men, with the ability to inspire people and renew their faith in life and humanity.' Another nurse, Dora Walker, who had been with the Hospital since early in 1917, later mentioned that Millie 'insisted that play should alternate with work, to ease the strain. We would come from the wards and find the guests that she had sent in, and we would dance to the gramophone till 12 o'clock.'

As so often in wartime, there were brief periods of intense activity when numbers of wounded had to be cared for, followed by days of hanging about with nothing much to do except wait for more news from the front. Katharine made great friends with the Duchess's daughter Rosemary Leveson-Gower, a fellow nurse, and they would sometimes go on nature rambles in the very pleasant surrounding countryside, untouched by war. French ill-treatment of their own civilians is a surprising element in her story.

Towards the end there were two great adventures. The first was when the much decorated war hero Bernard Freyberg gave them an experience of the trenches, which were situated in front of the British lines and not at all far from the Germans. Later there was another thrill when General Webb Bowen (an admirer of Rosemary's) arranged for the nurses to be taken, one at a time, for a joyride in the RFC's most advanced aeroplane, which Katharine described, lyrically, as an exhilarating experience, far superior to champagne and morphine.

At the end of August Katharine came home, mercifully before the epidemic of Spanish Flu set in, which caused more deaths in the wards, as elsewhere, than anything that had gone before.

KATHARINE ASQUITH'S

Rosemary Leveson-Gower with the Prince of Wales during a royal visit to No 9 Red Cross Hospital, 27 July 1917

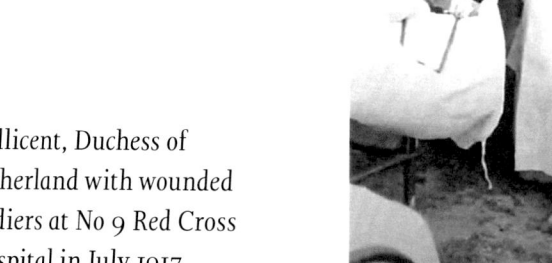

Millicent, Duchess of Sutherland with wounded soldiers at No 9 Red Cross Hospital in July 1917

The Diary which follows was kept by Katharine between April 1918 when she arrived at St Omer and late August 1918 when she returned home to England, as the so called Battle of Amiens unfolded, marking the final Allied offensive against the Germans which led to the conclusion of hostilities in November. Throughout her correspondence Katharine never accorded much concern for any regularity in her punctuation and dating, but we have tried to preserve as much as possible of her written text though sometimes we have made minor amendments for the sake of clarity. On a couple of occasions there remain some deeper ambiguities about her dating. The diary ends before her actual departure from the hospital. It is preserved in three lined exercise books (9" x 7"), housed until 1995 in Katharine's bedroom and now in the Mells Estate Archive. It provides clear evidence of both the nobility and the humility of her character, and the importance to her of literature, and above all of poetry.

John Jolliffe

The Diary

Katharine Asquith (second from left) in her ward

St Omer

WE ARRIVED HERE on Tuesday April 16th. Another day I doubt if we should have got through. Millie[1] had been ordered to evacuate her hospital on the Saturday but had prevailed on the authorities to let her stay on & open as a C.C.S. [Casualty Clearing Station]. Rosemary & I & one of the doctors travelled in great luxury to Boulogne & slept there & to our great relief in the morning found a car to take us on to St Omer. We were nervous as to our reception (Millie had sent a telephone message at the last moment to forbid our coming) but she didn't seem to mind much when we appeared. We live in a charming house—not roughing it at all as far as sleeping & eating goes. The hospital is in course of construction at the bottom of the garden. At present it is a sea of mud—huts being pieced together—all the nursing staff are there & a lot of doctors & orderlies. Everyone hard at work & over all the threat of being moved on if the battle goes badly & the Germans get any nearer. The other hospitals have all been sent away. The first day & night our guns sounded very near, but they are quieter now. There is a good deal to do for the French refugees who all pass through the town. They have emptied all the infirmaries & hospitals round & about & the French have made no provision for their people at all. The old ones die on the trains. Millie sent two of her nurses with a cattle truck full of paralytics who were being sent to Rouen & they have just come back telling dreadful stories of their experience & the brutality of the officials.

---

1   Millie/Milly: née Millicent St. Clair-Erskine (1867-1955). Married (1) Cromartie, 4th Duke of Sutherland; (2) 1914 Percy Fitzgerald; (3) 1919 George Hawes

My work is to help with the other VADs [Voluntary Aid Detachments] to get the huts ready. It is everything not having to sleep down there. The work is very hard for a little bit & then suddenly you can't find a job of any sort. I am cursed by my horrible self consciousness. It seems to get worse among all these strangers. Among the nurses & doctors I wonder if they dislike me or think I don't work hard enough because I live up here & don't really share their squalor when I am with Millie & Rosemary. I wish I had brought more practical but at the same time more becoming clothes. There is a Mrs Lischmann, the only other inhabitant of the chateau, whom I like. She is an American—divorced because her husband left her, very pretty & friendly & good. She is going to marry Alastair Leveson-Gower [the Duchess's younger son]. Millie & Rosemary have taken very kindly to her. It must be more embarrassing for her here than it is for me—but she is absolutely natural & unselfconscious.

I feel waves of loneliness & desperation though, all the time. I thank God that I have got here & don't at all want to leave. We all dread the order to evacuate which may come at any moment. Sometimes I hope we may be shelled in order that my distaste of living which it is good manners to conceal in everyday life may turn out to my advantage. If we are—& I don't expect we shall be—I suppose I shall be as frightened as anyone else.

I had a letter from Conrad [an early friend of Raymond. After the War he made completely unsuccesful attempts to marry Katharine] today, rather a surprise. It was a very sweet one—but gave me some uneasiness (a) because I think he likes me more than he had better (b) because he may try & come here.

I admire Millie more than I ever did before. Her zest & efficiency even if they are founded on egotism are remarkable. She thinks out everything even down to the vegetables & the safe storage of her war trophies. She cajoles & bullies just at the right moment. Her great idea is to have a large & beautiful hospital close to the firing line. One asks oneself why. I suppose it is the will to live which I can't recapture but I fully believe that no-one without her particular combination of beauty, position, urbanity & insensitiveness could have got it going & stayed here

I haven't taken any morphia since I arrived here.

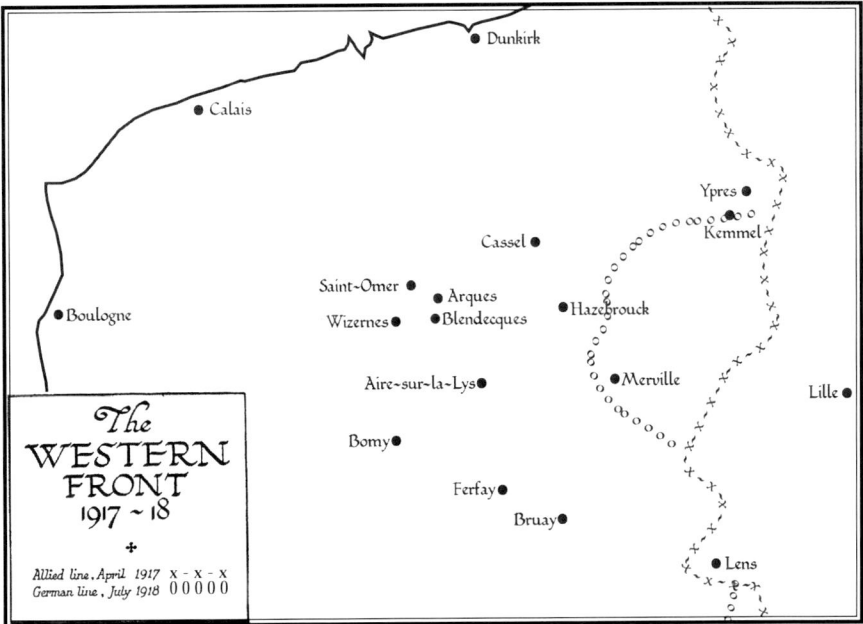

This is enough for a first entry of a diary. My mind oscillates oddly between thinking of my practical needs—wishing I had brought another pair of boots or a mackintosh apron—& thinking of Raymond & E [her brother Edward Horner who had been killed in November 1917] & the desert that has been made for my mind. Odd—I don't think much about the children. I thought that would distract me terribly. It's because I imagine them well.

Thursday April 18th
No change in our prospects here. The papers do not come but we heard on the telephone that the communique today told nothing. The line is still the same. Wild rumours that we picked up at the station last night about the retaking of Merville by the English seem to be untrue. We took down coats & blankets to an old paralytic woman of 82 who had been turned out of Eblingen at 5 minutes notice absolutely unprovided for. Rose & I went down at about 8 o'clock when the train was due & explored carriage after carriage in search of her. When we had succeeded & were propping her with pillows & blankets—all this in the dark with a host of other screaming, chattering, destitute old women all round her—a French official

came up & tried to turn them out of the carriage because it was 1st class instead of 3rd. We thwarted him & he went away muttering "Au moins il faut qu'elles payent le supplement". It was so insanely irrelevant that the phrase has become one of our maxims.

Milly had a bad fit of nerves this evening. I don't wonder as she is overstrained but it was rather queer. She talked about her mentality a good deal & argued very hotly that Rosemary must go away as soon as the shelling began. She also refused to let Rosemary smoke though they both do it all day. She thinks the eyes of the whole army besides all England are focussed on her hospital & that she cannot conduct it efficiently unless she is freed from all maternal responsibilities. Rosemary is equally determined to stay. I put in a plea for the liberty of the younger generation but only did myself harm. "It is all very well for me as I set out from the beginning to be the Great Worker of the war"

I wondered if we should all lose our reason here but I expect she was always a bit like that. After Milly had gone to bed, Rose, Mrs. L & I stayed up talking. I undertook the defence of Diana [Diana Manners, who married Duff Cooper after the War]. It is oddly difficult to explain her to the uninitiated. I did her no good except in so far as a strong confession of faith from an intelligent human being must do anyone good.

Shall we be turned adrift again or not? That is my chief preoccupation. This is the most dramatic place to be in—one is so secluded in the middle of all the devastation. I have a great panic about my efficiency as a V.A.D when the patients come if they ever do. All the rest look so hard bitten & competent

Saturday April 20th
I have been alone all this afternoon. The VADs and sister were given a free afternoon because for the moment there is nothing to do in the huts. Millie, Rose & Mrs Lischmann have gone to Boulogne. Mrs Lischmann looked so happy—she was going to see Alastair Leveson-Gower who gets leave to meet her there. I tried to remember what it was like to be as happy as that. I walked down to the town & looked at the cathedral & wrote some letters & now I am reading *Resurrection* which makes a great impression on me. I cannot criticize it as a book,

I just read it as doctrine. It frightens & consoles & yet very often I feel it doesn't face the real arguments in defence of this order. No one ever puts them & all acquiescent people are made stupid & bloated. I have a lovely view of the cathedral from this window. Just now there has been a slanting ray on the tower & now it has gone out.

I wonder if keeping a diary is a way of showing off. I suppose it is. I have a horror of showing off revived in me by Milly. Sybil was my old danger post in that way. How strange to find a link between such different lives. I suppose I join on too, only I hope I'm not so blatant about it. This morning I woke up and cried for Raymond. I haven't done that for a long time—one gets numb at home but being with new people is like having a second amputation. I was tempted to take morphia this afternoon to beguile the time & make me write easily but it didn't seem quite worth while. Partly I am a little afraid of the way it affects me when I am alone but partly my beautiful σωφροσυνη² hinders me. Or is it apathy. I like to think of myself as poised & self controlled. I don't distrust my will but I don't think my temptations are quite frantic enough to make it remarkable

Sunday April 21st
We had gas mask drill today which was rather funny. I shall try to preserve my mask as a curio.

Colonel Black & Harry Graham to luncheon. They say a big German attack is imminent, both here and further south. A wonderful post. Letters from Mother, Diana, Duff & Bluey [Harold Baker]. Diana's made me sad—she was in revolt against her life, & Mother's too sounded anxious & sad. I feel angry with Con for not making her go to the wedding. How terribly stupid people are even about their great friends.

I think Milly dislikes me, anyhow she isn't the least nice to me which makes it embarrassing to be here, but one will notice this sort of thing less when work begins. I cannot bear that feeling of indifference coloured with hostility even in people like Milly whom I don't much esteem. It always fills me with surprise & dismay & impedes my unsteady self confidence.

---

2 'sophrosune'—A Greek virtue combining prudence and general wisdom

Diana complained of Venetia's "side squint for her prompt" which made me laugh.

I copy out a piece of *Resurrection* which I thought painfully applicable to me: 'All people live & act partly under the influence of their own thoughts and partly under the influence of the thoughts of others. One of the chief distinctions between people is determined by how much they live according to their own ideas or those of others—some people, the majority, use their own thoughts as a mental toy or treat their reason as a flywheel from which the driving belt has been taken off, while in their acts they submit to thoughts of others, to custom, tradition, law—others again regard their own ideas as the prime movers of all their actions'. It is awkwardly put but I find the bit about the flywheel very just.

Tuesday April 23rd
I've very little to write but I am so afraid of losing the diary habit that I have to go on recording nothing. I think I was fanciful about Milly disliking me. She began to talk to me about her marriage which I took as a compliment though I dare say she has a great many confidants. She seems to be thoroughly disillusioned & regards it very sensibly as a mistake which must be retrieved with as much dignity as possible but which she cannot allow to destroy her life. She is full of unflagging courage. I marvel at it in one so much older than me. Every week diminishes mine. We dined with General Ponsonby at Wizernes. He commands the 40th Division now. I had the best place at dinner between him and his GSO1, a certain Colonel Black. I wanted to talk to him [Ponsonby] as Raymond loved him so—but Milly naturally had the first claim on him & Black, a terribly intense man, entangled me in most solemn topics. My style was a good deal cramped by Rosemary who was struggling with the ADCs & I find it dreadfully difficult to understand the General. The whole dinner was rather a touching affair. They had a band & marvellous food in a little sort of workhouse close to the canal.

The Division has just come out to rest there after terrible fighting. I suppose a dinner party was rather an unusual event for them as it was for us. I kept thinking of Raymond who used to like dining with him when he commanded their brigade & often wrote to tell me about it. I never thought that I should be doing it instead.

I dreamt of Raymond last night, a silly dream about his being terribly late for dinner—never coming down & all of us wondering why & getting a little angry. But in the morning when I woke up I thought of the dream as an asset, though such a poor one. Yet for a little while I had believed him to be alive.

Sunday April 28th
Yesterday we spent in Boulogne marrying Alastair Leveson-Gower & Helene. It was half pitiful, half farcical. I felt too detached to appreciate either. They were married at 5.30 in a funny little English church with about half a dozen officers, one or two of us from the hospital in our grimmest uniforms & Lady Hadfield & Lady Algernon Gordon Lennox dressed as for a London wedding, the former in pure white. Then a rather difficult hour of sitting about making conversation, & then a bridal dinner which was indescribably pathetic. Helene looked a darling but there was no one but Rose who could put any heart into our fiddling, & the oddly assorted 14 who sat down to dinner were too much for her for all her braveness. We brought them cowslips and champagne from the hospital—but not quite enough champagne & the only person who got at all drunk was our CO Captain Morgan. He sat next me but it was barely noticeable even to my trained eye. We drove back here after dinner, 50 kilometres in a cold white mist and an open car. I rather enjoyed it until I got stiff & cold. Captain Morgan sat on my feet & gave me the cramp & we lost our way.

Today work in the hospital, carrying mattresses, fitting screens together etc, Colonel Black to tea, Colonel Shute to dinner…Milly was in bed & I persuaded her to receive them both which she did very willingly & thereby relieved me of a good deal of their entertainment. As a matter of fact they were both quite nice men. There has been a good deal of gun firing today in the distance. They say Kemmel has gone but they have said it for some days past now. If we don't retake it it will mean leaving the Ypres salient [it was retaken in September]. I had a little note from Trotter telling of some of the places that Raymond frequented here. I was glad to get it.

We are to take in patients on Tuesday. I am sent to G & H ward. It might be worse. I am getting into a panic about my capacity.

I read *Macbeth* & some of *Othello* & also some of Morley's *Gladstone*

Duff has gone to France but where Heaven only knows. I ache for Diana, she must be so lonely.

I wrote some letters for Milly today. She was in bed & dictated them. In each she put "These are very anxious days". Her unselfconsciousness is stupefying.

Monday April 29th
Today Rose & I motored up to Ebblingem to the refugee camp to fetch back two of our Sisters who had been lent to them & to distribute clothes. It is much nearer the line than this—almost the last railhead. The road was covered with French troops hurrying up chiefly guns & transport but we got through in our ambulance unchallenged. The place we got to haunts me now. There was a big camp with tents, not very full as it happens but terribly bleak & desolate, & a little improvised hospital at the top of the hill where we found our two sisters & some French nuns—working for most pitiful cases. Old women who had left everything behind & hadn't even a bundle of rags, & a consumptive girl who cried & begged us to take her back as she didn't mind the shells & was sure this place would kill her in a worse way. When I came in Sister Gleve was washing a baby of a fortnight old who had been left there by a girl of eighteen. She wasn't married & had gone back to fetch her other child evidently not intending to return. There was a dead man in a bed close to a little child of ten or so & the French nuns proceeded to strip the body & roll it up in a blanket in front of us all without a screen or any covering to hide what was going on from the other patients. Rose carried away the child to another bed but that was all we could do. The woman in charge of the place, a horrible smart Frenchwoman called Madame Lioville (suspected of being in the Secret Service) came in while this was going on & grumbled at them for taking away a blanket from the living as they had so few! It seemed a nightmare. They were pathetically grateful for the clothes which we brought with us but it was difficult to understand most of the people as they spoke Flemish. The afternoon we spent hard

at work in hospital, as we have our first convoy tomorrow & E ward wasn't ready.

A Captain Elwes to dinner—highly recommended by Milly & Helene who have the worst possible taste in men, & rather a failure with Rose & me who have the best possible. I'm half asleep as I write this & rather frightened about tomorrow.

Monday May 6th
I haven't written for a week out of pure laziness. The first two days of being in the ward made me so tired & after that the routine becomes simply dull. In the first place we had quite light cases. In the second I have a very bad sister, the worst in the hospital, not ill natured but muddle headed, rather contradictory, rather vain & <u>very</u> difficult to work with. She is known for this thro'out the hospital. Her name is Dempster. She is old & a mulatto. She rather likes me because I am deferential & interested in the Fabian Society of which she is a member. I shall never mention her again & seize the first opportunity of leaving her ward. I may be able to effect this when the night duty changes but it may be difficult. The sister of the adjoining ward is called Maxwell-Stuart. She lived at Traquair—it belongs to her uncle—she is very nice. Her V.A.D is called Kennedy, rather competent, quite dull. Sister Dempster has me and Walker as she has the most cases to deal with at present. Walker is pale, quite young, one of a family of ten. She works hard but the others don't like her much. I get on with her admirably—in fact I can get on with them all. There is something odd about Walker: she reads. She was once a Sunday school teacher. One day the men were playing some new tunes on the gramophone & were delighted by a particularly vulgar song. Walker went calmly up to the instrument, took the record & broke it in two & then took the two pieces to the sister. It was the bravest thing I have ever known. I didn't see it myself (it happened before I came) but I gather the whole hospital regarded it as an outrage & bullied & punished & ragged her (including the authorities).

These are the people I see every day. We begin work at eight. While the cases are light there isn't much to do after the first two or three hours of scrubbing & tidying, & my sister lets me off a good deal. Anyway you get two clear hours off in the afternoon or evening & plenty of time for meals. If there were a rush my ward would do badly as Dempster has no method. Yesterday we had a trying evening but were asked to dine with the 51st division—the most famous of all the territorials. It is supposed to be the only division that the Germans fear as much as the Guards. It is entirely Scotch & mostly Highland Scotch. They were resting about eight miles from here, just beyond Aire (Aire-sur-la-Lys) a lovely name & lovely in its church. They sent the General's motor for us & Milly after forbidding us to mention the expedition in our letters consented to go. The division was going back into the line the very next day & most of them had already started. Only the General & his staff & comedians remained behind. They had a troupe of follies who were going to give a performance for us. It was a stiff affair. I had sat at dinner between the General & the GSOI. The General was a small, rather intelligent looking man but dry & tired. I found a topic with the GSO by discovering that he had been a schoolboy at Clifton—rather a disappointment as far as local colour went but I was never much caught by Scotch sentiment! There was lots of champagne but my head was too good for the amount that I thought it advisable to drink. After dinner we were taken to a little school room rigged up with a stage & sat through the most nightmarish performance. Very up to date vulgar songs all written by the staff! A male impersonator—a curate!—everyone frightfully keen & enthusiastic & watching to see if we were amused. It went down all right with Milly & Rose & I clapped till my hands ached. Then supper [sic] more champagne & "our last night" till I was half crying. Then a long drive home along rainwashed roads & stars & the guns making flashes like summer lightning all over the sky. There were Verey lights & great noises in the distance—we were really only a very little way from the trenches & I thought that now I was seeing something of what Raymond & E must have seen every night only I was in a motor going along an absolutely safe road & they had been tired & near the shells. It is difficult to describe the sort of mystery that the night & the flashes in that very quiet country threw over the whole situation. And then I absolutely broke down. The future seemed so impossible & the longing so violent. I cried all the way home. I suppose it was partly reaction from the effort of the evening—luckily Milly & Rose fell asleep & never knew. Crying too makes one sleepy & I went to bed feeling quite dazed & stupid—& then the bloody nightingales began & I thought about "To thy high requiem become a sod" & who more truly than I.

Tuesday May 7th
Last night [sic] we had General Kennedy of the 9th Division (I think he is only a brigadier) & Colonel Hadow & another Captain to dinner. There was bridge—Milly & I & the General left out. I might have gone to bed but it was difficult as Milly had complained in front of the company of how Rosemary & I always disappeared when there were visitors who bored us & left them on her hands. She was very angry with Rose for playing bridge as apparently Kennedy is eligible & didn't play. She is <u>mad</u> for Rosemary to marry. They have extraordinarily funny talks about it, in fact when we are alone we talk of nothing else. Milly attributes her failure to 'get off' to two chief causes:

(a) her money—to which I demur

(b) her lack of sentiment

She entreats her to assume a little interest in 'abstract topics' as a lure. I doubt that sort of bird lime myself, but certainly it is Milly's own strategy & you might as well ask Rosemary to learn *Paradise Lost* by heart or translate Racine into English alexandrines. I adore Rose—she is the only girl after Diana whom I would give a fig to marry if I were a man. She has a beautiful figure, pure truthfulness of character & perfect taste. Her truthfulness & taste are very remarkable. She has no poses or *arrière pensée*—everything is natural in her & she is full of generosity & fair mindedness & on top of this simplicity she has a kind of flair which makes her enjoy *Zuleika Dobson* rather more than Philips Oppenheim though she reads both with zest—& nothing in between the two—which makes her love the same people that I love & discard nearly all the bores (except Hélène) & never say or do a foolish or embarrassing thing.

I pin in here a letter from Belloc which I adored getting but answered with great difficulty & one from Ettie to Rosemary which I thought rather funny [neither has survived].

Tonight Black, Harry Graham & Saner dined. I filled my usual role being the one left out from bridge, but tonight I avoided wrecking Milly's tête à tête with Black for whom she has a weakness & escaped up here. The bombardment began again today very heavily—probably somewhere beyond Hazebrouck. There was a rumour a few days ago that the French wanted to take over the whole of our northern line & send the whole English army to the south but I gather we have resisted the scheme. Everyone says that the French gave up Kemmel without a blow but fought very well afterwards.

I have been reading Gilbert Murray's translation of *The Bacchae* with a good deal of pleasure. I tried to learn some of it by heart. It isn't quite good enough for that but it is fine reading after the ward work.

Friday May 17th
I have left too long a time elapse since I wrote which makes it terribly difficult to begin again.

I've had a relapse about muffy. I started by taking it last Saturday 11th because we had a dance in the house for Alastair & Hélène & I couldn't face it unaided. Only a few soldiers & V.A.Ds & it was all over in a couple of hours. I didn't mind it as much as I anticipated owing to the detachment I secured. The next day Sunday we spent in the lily wood, Alastair, Hélène, Rose & I. It was a divine day but wasted on us—we four could only sit in the wood & cap bad rhymes, lamentably bad ones. Then A told two or three amazingly dirty stories which we laughed at to show we weren't shocked. I could have cried over my solitariness, servileness & general sense of incompetence to hew anything like a life out of my circumstances. And they aren't such bad circumstances either. I rather liked Alastair in spite of his limitations.

When we got home we found 12 people sitting round the table—but Milly took away the Generals & left us to cope with the riff raff. Then there was a crisis—a telegram arrived to say that Fitzgerald[3] had arrived in Paris! Poor Milly she faced it very well & went off to Paris on the Tuesday. She told me a lot about her marriage in the

---

3   Percy Desmond Fitzgerald (11th Hussars), whom Milly had married (2nd husband) in October 1914

interval between the telegram & her departure & I hedged rather & said I admired her all the more for having done it & that she must dispose of it without regret which I think she is quite prepared to do.

I took another dose quite wantonly on Monday—simply because I wasn't well & saw a chance of avoiding hospital & lying in bed the next day. The mere fact of not having to get up in the morning was irresistible. The same thing has happened tonight. It wouldn't do for London life & I have a twinge or two of self distrust which I must quench by a period of abstinence.

I spent that Monday night in reading Knox's book[4]—disappointedly. It is rather queer & chic in these times to write a whole book to explain why you change from the Anglican to the Catholic church, especially when like Knox you have adopted every Catholic tenet long before you took the step, but I wanted to know why he was a clergyman or indeed a Christian at all & of that there is not a hint given. The book was simply a question of labels & I thought the title a little pompous. I suppose it seemed a long journey to him but he failed to convey the impression of one even to a sympathetic reader. One saw the goal before one had read two lines & nothing at all about Dido.

I have had a grim week of depression, perhaps the result of the morphia, partly at any rate the result of nothing to do. I have about 10 cases in the ward but all quite light ones & I'm terribly bored with Dempster & Walker. I have to be there a good deal though I'm bound to say Sister is quite nice about letting me off. The heat has been wonderful but I can hardly bear to work in it & my clothes are all unsuitable.

On Saturday a luncheon picnic with General Kennedy & Colonel Hadow in the lily wood—another profanation of my favourite place & a terribly dusty drive in an ambulance to 9th Division sports. Today at my lowest ebb two good things happened. Maurice[5] came to luncheon & I had a fine letter from Diana. I could have cried for joy at seeing Maurice—it made me realise how homesick I had been for the past just to see someone who knew about it. I got little good from it really

---

4   Probably *A Spiritual Aeneid*
5   Maurice Baring, a much valued friend, then in the Royal Flying Corps

as Philip Sassoon was there all the time (Rose in bed) but I gave them luncheon & wished Maurice well as I've never done before.

There was a tremendous air raid the night before last, the worst I've known yet, but Rose & I gave each other a fine display of nerve. I truly felt very little afraid & was relieved to note it. However it may be the test was not a very searching one as the bombs were a good way off. Tonight I talked about dying & about marrying to Rose & worked myself up to a glimpse of the right attitude about all the important awful things. *To live from fear set free, to breathe and wait, To hold a hand uplifted over hate* [Euripides, The Bacchae]. I wish I could keep at that point but I only get for a few seconds at a time.

Monday May 20th
Last night the worst air raid I've ever been in. I can quite honestly record that I didn't feel one single tremor. I dare say one's nerve would wear out but at present the fuss which the others make is a mystery to me. Is it lack of imagination or simply the will to die? Both probably. I really don't somehow believe that I should have minded much in pre-war days. Rose who has every temptation to live and a great grip on pleasure is just like me so I suppose we both have rather sluggish emotions. The doctors were [?up] all night but I was rather shocked at everyone else. One man, the Quartermaster, went about with a tin hat on tearfully imploring the nurses to take their white caps off in case it should attract fire. I shall never forget the scene when Milly at last plucked up courage to go down to the camp after sitting with me for an hour in pitch darkness, wincing at every report. Rose was out when it started. I did feel very frightened about her as I pictured her dashing along in a motor through the bombs & thought what a terrible pity it would be if anything happened, always the best people are fated. I didn't dare talk about her to Milly for fear she was suffering from the same ghastly preoccupation but suddenly I realized that it had never crossed her mind. She was bothered about the hospital. When there seemed to be a lull we wandered down there. The moonlight was as clear as day, but in the south east the sky was rose coloured. A great ammunition dump had been fired near Arques and the blaze was wonderfully lovely. The searchlight made long white beams across the clear sky & the noise was

simply terrific. It was the most exciting moment—the beauty of the sky & the noise & the horror far off combined to put an edge on the most trivial & familiar thoughts. There were a great many machine guns firing & bombs dropping & every now & then a great explosion from the dump. It lasted till four but at about one I went to bed as I felt that nothing was going to happen. This morning everyone in a great flutter & the same boring remarks from each person you meet.

I've read Bosanquet *Suggestions on Ethics*. It rather impressed me, in bits irritated me too. The bit about punishment is a good antidote to *Resurrection*—a totally different point of view & more convincing.

Friday May 24th
We had two or three more nights of air raids—but none so sensational as the 19th. I didn't lie awake for them though one heard the German aeroplanes quite plainly. There was no barrage, but a new plan of only sending up our machines to pursue them. You heard nothing but the engines of the aeroplanes & a certain amount of machine gun fire.

Wednesday was the hottest day of the year. I felt quite sick in our ward—luckily there wasn't much to do, but in the afternoon one could scarcely breathe. I sat there till about five & then a little tremulously set out for a walk with Elsie Haldane. I had promised to go with her to the wood & was ashamed to cry off but the expedition was a success. The air & the exercise revived me & the wood as usual was divine. Colonel Black came to dinner. We had a rather dead rubber of bridge—no-one but Rose could have got it going as Black hated it & wanted to talk about his soul to Milly or me & I was dead tired but on the whole thought it less effort than conversation.

That night the Germans dropped bombs on No.10 Stationary in the town & wrecked it, so yesterday they sent us all their patients. The hospital started into life quite unprepared in spite of weeks of gestation. We had 80 patients in during the afternoon, some very near death. I was transferred to A ward this morning. It is the nearest ward to the theatre, so we have some of the worst cases there. The sister is very efficient, her name Scally, Irish, rather old with short grey hair.

Almack the V.A.D is very ungraceful but good natured & competent.

They didn't really want me much & I have suffered from a derelict feeling all day. My old ward had filled up too but there was very little to do there. I was glad to change but one feels terribly awkward in a new ward & at a loss. I believe I'm hopelessly unsuited to hospital work, too slow & too sad. There is no one so useless in the place except perhaps my old mulatto, Dempster, & she has got the sack.

I began to write a poem last night but suppose I shan't ever finish it—a comparison of myself to Lot's wife.

Milly got a bit on my nerves. A good deal of talk about her mentality. The war affords her such tremendous scope for 'being beautiful' & when I'm tired it maddens me. I'm afraid I let a little of it out to Hélène which was most unwise.

Rose has been a slave to the theatre. Luckily on the very day when we filled up the weather broke, It is cold & wet with rain which is depressing but makes one less tired & more likely to get sleep. I slept very ill during the heat but didn't dare make my nights happy because of being up early.

Sunday May 26th
Two days of grinding work since I last wrote. My inefficiency continues to be very marked, but I have been too exhausted to care for anything. I am terribly grateful for being so tired—it's as good as muffy & more honourable—or is that just that I know that I oughtn't to be in a war hospital but yet I really like [it?]. In the morning I'm sick with fright, the foreknowledge that I shall botch the primus & drop the wet gauze & fumble with it & hand the wrong forceps & fail to clean the tubes & sicken at the smell of Daken[6] & then I get hotter & tireder & my feet ache & the evening looms nearer & becomes a blissful prospect & my mind becomes quite numb, too dull for any regrets or anticipations & I just feel a certain relief & happiness over food & cigarettes & the coolness of sheets.

We turned out all our cases today, some were very bad, far too bad for the journey but all except one embarking on it joyfully for the sake of going home. I nearly cried as I pinned them up in their blankets, two a piece brown ones incredibly thick & dirty, but that is an army regulation, so it doesn't matter how hot they are, & watched

---

6   The 'Carrel Dakin technique' for treating bacteria on wounds

them jolting away in awful breathless ambulances with dust eddying around them. Mr Schlesinger has become the doctor in the ward this week, he is much the best. Milly summed him up rather well as a minor Winston. He is a real bounder, but very quick & dexterous, exacting but not unreasonable to the nurses, perfect to the patients, ridiculously egotistic but devoid of cant.

An air raid has just started and Milly has hustled Helene & Rose off to a dug out trench. I am so tired I hope it won't be a bad one.

Sunday June 2nd
I can't believe it is so long since I wrote. I've quite settled down in my ward. I adore Scally & have established friendly relations with Almack. The work has been fluctuating, some days very heavy & tiring, some days not enough to do. It's cooler which makes a difference. I know now where things are kept, I understand the slinging a Daken, I've conquered the A ward primus & a blue obedient flame leaps up when I breathe upon it.

Yesterday was my half day. We had planned to entertain the V.A.Ds & doctors at tea on the lawn to commemorate the mention of two of them in despatches & afterwards to dine ourselves with Kennedy & Hadow (who had been over to dinner the day before) on top of Cassel Hill some ¾ hour from here which would have been very interesting. It is fairly near the line & commands a wonderful view (Kennedy seems to indulge an unreciprocated fancy for Rose). Alas two disasters bitched every plan. 'Fitz' turned up in the middle of the V.A.Ds' party & as if that were not enough a convoy of Americans who had been blown to bits by a bombing accident arrived 10 minutes later. Rose was hurried off to the theatre & Milly was left supported by Helène & me to face her husband. While we were still gasping Sir Arthur Lawley[7] chose to drop in for a cup of tea.

I saw the entertainment of the staff through & then deserted the house & took a long solitary walk to the Blandec wood. I had a sudden craving for exercise & walked myself stiff. When I came in I found that Helène had thrown up the sponge & retired to bed. Rose was still operating on the Yankees & I was left to dine with Milly & Fitz. A more desperate meal has never passed my lips. Milly was incapable

---

7 British colonial administrator and a Red Cross Commissioner in WW1

of speech, what Fitzgerald's feelings were I could not fathom but he seemed by turns ill tempered & defiantly at ease. I chattered like a cricket. I tried every topic—the Zionist movement (he had just come back from Palestine), Newmarket (he was a friend of Cicely's & George's), the Pretty Lady & finally steered triumphantly into harbour with the Maud Allan libel action which lasted us satisfactorily enough until I thought it decent to leave them to their tête à tête. I knew Milly dreaded it but she had got to face it sooner or later & as the night was wearing on I judged it better for her sake (& for mine) that it should be sooner. The upshot of it all is still hidden from me, though the first moment I am alone with Milly the desire to discuss it will rend her very filmy reserve, but he departed before luncheon today. I was really terribly sorry for Milly. I had judged her to be a person without any but purely artificial emotions. She seemed to me yesterday to be quite overwhelmed by the situation, no mask at all—it was pathetic to see someone of her experience taken by surprise & behaving like an oppressed child. I dare say there is something to be said on Fitzgerald's side too but I didn't take to him. The way he moved his shoulders made me sick.

I had a sweet letter from Duff today. He has been posted to Raymond's battalion [in the Grenadiers] & told me how the few survivors of the Somme adored his memory still. A new ensign came to the battalion called Raymond & they wouldn't call him that but had to invent an obscene nickname at once to obviate the necessity. They said that there had never been anyone so unmoved in danger but that I knew. The thought of Raymond's courage is one of the things that can still give me a feeling of pure joy. It affects me quite oddly and irrationally. Sometimes I believe it was the quality I most loved in him but then I think of others that really matter far more. I don't quite know why this particular one creates such an emotion in me. Lots of people are brave but not quite in the same way. I dreamt of him so clearly the night before last. I woke up again saying to myself at least I have had something but it's no use for it's only my idea of him, & I don't want a creature of my own brain.

On my solitary walk I meditated writing a poem about this. I thought of a side allusion to morphia in it. A lover takes a draught from a witch as a last desperate means of evoking the dead but finds it has shortened the stature of his soul. I don't suppose I shall get it done.

I had a sweet letter from Diana. I cling to the thought of her.

I read Gibbon's autobiography with a good deal of pleasure; also a tolerable novel called *The Crescent Moon*, like Conrad without the bite.

Bluey writes me the most approved love letters every day—I can hardly bear it. Diana says he is entirely wrecked by brandy. He still has nothing to do & in my absence his attachment to me becomes almost hysterical. When I go back he will loathe me after a week. Letters from home have been rather intermittent. Gibbon kept a journal in French at immense length. How do people keep it up? I miss out all the tiny funny things that happen & which it would be fun to recall afterwards & only remember to write at long intervals with great difficulty. I also miss out really important public events. No one would imagine from tonight's entry that for the past week the most deadly and important battle of the war has been raging round Soissons. But while the fighting is so far south we only get official news & that late. Everyone is frightened but no-one knows anything. One might be in England. The nearer we get to the scene of action the more sluggish the imagination becomes. It takes a bomb in the garden now to convince me of an air raid. The last three nights have been peaceful.

Wednesday June 5th
I had a very tiring day in the ward yesterday. Almack was off. A man died of gas gangrene. There were two evacuations & a heavy dressing all to be coped with simultaneously. The death affected me not at all at the time. I scarcely knew the man, he had only been in 24 hours—the case was hopeless from the first—& he was an Italian American which seems to me a bad combination. We have a lot of Americans here now & I'm rather insular about them. Afterwards in the night the town of Arques was shelled—as I lay in bed waiting for the sound of the shells bursting—one came every 7 minutes—the picture of that poor deathbed had rather a depressive effect on me. It was so squalid. No-one cared a bit, but it wasn't that. It was the way he lay in bed, the horrible breathing, the colour of him. I talked about it to Almack this morning to try & get it off my mind, but

apparently it outrages a nurse's sense of decency to talk about death at all. I've noticed this before & it always strikes me as funny.

Saturday June 7th
Last night we were shelled as before or rather Arques at a great distance was shelled. I couldn't sleep at all as I had had a half day & drowsed all through the afternoon. I was still haunted by that deathbed. To see someone die however familiar one is with the idea of death gives one a certain trembling of the knees. This is going to happen to me—perhaps soon, anyway sometime. It has happened to the only person I loved. It's only a question of nerves, I really don't fear the idea of my death at all. How could I? I can think of nothing in life that will give me any happiness. I think I shall feel a moment of great expectation & pleasure when I see the children again, especially Trim & it would be very pleasant to spend a night talking to Diana & reacting to each other, but I do not cling so very passionately to these anticipations so they are the best that the future holds. But I do hope death won't be horrible like No. 20's, among overworked worried people who have to put on gloves to touch the bedclothes. I have a feeling that I was somehow found wanting that afternoon. [page torn out]

… The General himself is a completely neutral figure still in my mind. Though I talked to him for an hour I could discover no attributes except that he was tall & interested in his profession. I took a good dose of muffy to get me through so complicated an evening, which perhaps obscured my perceptions. Hélène is so incurably romantic that though she knows she was the victim of a hoax she has not relinquished hope. It shows how little people who see one every day can know about one.

   The 15th is now the day given for the big German attack

   I finished Gibbon & am now reading an admirable book called *Eminent Victorians* by Lytton Strachey, It's most ironical & very well done.

Thursday June 13th
Work has been very slack since last week. Alastair Leveson-Gower came over for Sunday. As usual the contrast between Hélène's lot &

General Thomas Ince Webb Bowen

mine seemed very forcible. There is something pathetically bridal about her when these meetings take place. He is just a funny but she rather reminds me of myself at eighteen though I think I must have been even then more complicated & much less attractive.

On Sunday Webb Bowen, Immecour, Gen. Ponsonby & others came to tea, & the three young people took refuge in Milly's hut leaving Milly & me to entertain the party. I took more trouble than usual & in consequence exchanged about three sentences with General Webb Bowen, a nice but very silent man during the meal. It was enough. Milly's eagle eye detected the sacred spark lurking in the smoke of those commonplace remarks & she & Helene in the incredible simplicity & perhaps sweetness of their natures have evolved an elaborate plan of working up an affaire de coeur between us. Rose of course overcome by merriment revealed it to me & implored me to rag them a little about it. I swear I did very little but my success almost frightened me. They now refuse to believe the grim truth. Last night he was asked to dinner & very palpable manoeuvres left us tête à tête. It is really too much of a shame but the light it threw on Milly's & Helene's minds was the thing that startled me. They made me rock with laughter. They made me feel incredibly insulted.

I was callous & at the same time morbidly observant in fact I was damnable. I hope writing this will exorcise the memory. I don't want another night of it.

We had Wigam & Ruthven to dinner & played bridge afterwards. I rather liked them. Wigam seemed the more intelligent, but though better looking his face reminded me slightly of McKenna's.

Today has been a slack day in the ward—only five patients left. I am not required early tomorrow so I have given myself a stab & am looking forward to a perfect night & morning.

Saturday June 15th
An idle day. Rose in bed with influenza. She & Milly are quite crazy about health. Rose lies in bed looking I admit rather ill & taking her temperature every ¼ of an hour. It's never more than 99. They swallow millions of potions, every quack medicine under the sun has its vogue & then are deeply surprised at feeling ill. I laugh a good deal at Rose but take Milly *au grand serieux*. There are only two patients in the ward.

I had my usual budget of letters. 3 from Bluey, 1 from Conrad & one to my joy from Duff saying he could come here in the course of the next two or three days. Alas I fear he will be stopped. Harry Graham has just come in with news that has confirmed a rumour from the aerodrome which reached us earlier in the afternoon. He says there is a concentration of the Germans near Hazebrouck & his Division the 40th has been ordered to be ready to go into the line. It looks bad as the 40th Div is in process of reconstruction & consists at present of some Chinese Labour Battalions who have never seen a rifle till today & some very unfit B men who arrived yesterday from England & couldn't possibly march as far as Hazebrouck. It may be a false alarm but Harry was terribly rattled. We gave him a bottle of champagne & a very good dinner to steady him & now we begin to listen for ambulances. If this bit of the line is as unprepared as Harry says it seems they would do well to attack. We shall either get some work or have to move homewards. I hope Duff will get his visit in first.

Tuesday June 18th
No work no offensive no Duff—something really ought to be coming our way. I am in a state of depression: *Der eine sprach wie weh wird mir* and so on. Last night an indescribable scene between Milly & Rose. I played the part of Patroclus dead, but my position was something

more delicate than that of a literally dead body. Milly discovered Rose's betrayal of the Webb Bowen scheme & indulged in the most fantastic flights of Rhetoric. It was all muddled up with a bet of £50 to £1 which they had made about my future & the fact that Rose never falls in love herself. She accused Rose in turn of cupidity & cynicism & celibacy till if I had been her I should have screamed & run out of the house but Rose's form was perfect. She sat there calmly enough indulging in an occasional quip & an occasional protest. The *comble* came when Milly said the want of reticence & sensitiveness in the younger generation made her ill—this after the whole tirade in my presence about my possible *engouement* for a man whom I had only sat next to once at tea at a time when I am completely knocked out for the rest of my natural life. It was really funny enough & the oddest part of all was that you couldn't but rather love Milly all through it. She is such a child, meant so well & is so terribly encumbered by a daughter. But I could hardly believe my ears. I am thinking that I shall go mad unless I get something to do. Failing that, the influenza is the best I can hope for. I took my temperature hopefully this morning (I am catching the habit of the family) & found it disappointingly normal. Everyone here has had it except me.

I read the *Eve of St Mark*. I wish Keats had finished it. I've also learnt by heart Hamlet's speech *How all occasions do inform against me* which just lasts me down the road to the hospital. Duff said in his letter that Diana had sent him my two poems which he liked. I was rather pleased at this because she never answered my letter in which I sent them. I thought they must have embarrassed her too much. Now I think she couldn't have taken quite that view as she wouldn't deliberately do me in with Duffy. I stick in the poems here.

> Be merciful sweet Time spread all thy years
> Between my grief and me, make me a mask
> O skilful Time that nobody may ask
> Of this changed aspect & these fruitless tears
> Thou art almighty even in our last beliefs
> Canst melt the mountains & make dark the sun
> Thou who has trampled out a million griefs

Spare not this youngest most despairing one
But when I hear thy heavy & swift footfall
I do recant & utterly deny thee
I will not ask for any grace at all
But spurn thy hateful craft so passing by me
Leave thou my empty heart unsalved nor dry me
One single tear—O Time I did not call
How can I live as if you were not here
When in my ear
Your voice still echoes & each laughing word
Is held and heard
When I can taste in one remembered kiss
The whole of bliss
Only my eyes, traitor to you and me,
No longer see
There was a strange & bitter thing I know
Said long ago
By one most wise "Let the dead men", he said
"Bury the dead"

My ears are deaf, my lips are filled with dust
Come, as you must
Enter my eyes that I fulfil my need
And die indeed

Thursday June 20th
Last night we had a funny evening. To please Schlesinger Rose & I & Fleet (the theatre V.A.D, a dark passionate Canadian, rather like Hilda Moore to look at) dressed up in Rose's best evening dresses, dined & played at bridge. S. looked very queer in evening dress. This is ambiguous. <u>He</u> didn't wear one of Rose's dresses but a man's ordinary evening dress which he had procured with great difficulty from London to remind him of pre-war days. He is rather clever & sees more than most people. He told me that I had been ill 14 months ago & that I shall probably live till 70 which depressed me considerably. I couldn't sleep last night. Tomorrow we go to Dunkirk. I'm off duty for the day. xxx

Saturday June 22nd

We had a rather amusing day on Thursday [Friday]. I took a whole holiday from the ward—an unscrupulous measure which it will take some little while to live down especially as Rose behaved rather tactlessly & instead of letting me arrange it myself invoked matron's interference. Before starting we launched a somewhat indifferent parody of 'If' which we had composed the night before for Fleet's 'books' (all the sisters and V.A.Ds have 'books' full of signatures & humorous sketches) upon the theatre. It had a startling & unmerited success. Captain Chappell didn't know we had such brilliant wit in us. Then we set out by motor for Dunkirk. I was in that rather muted but extremely receptive & impressionable frame of mind which succeeds a dose of morphia. I remember speculating in the motor as to whether the drug was my master or my slave. In favour of the first is the fact that it destroys the will to act. I watch the world unfolding before me without bitterness or pain & indulge in alluring dreams of what I could write or say. Against its mastery & in favour of my being rather an exception in this respect is that I have no physical craving for it at all—my body & nerves don't want it & I have no reaction of bad spirits after taking it, at any rate not definitely or soon after. If I were to be deprived of it for ever I should only regret a possible source of pleasure in the future being cut off, just as if I were told I could never see a Shakespeare play or eat a strawberry again. From which I argue that it is my servant still & if treated judiciously may remain so.

We drove in the motor through a wonderful blue country, flat & open till we climbed Cassel Hill. Cassel is divine and baffles description—a little medieval town perched very high on the summit of the steepest hill in the world with marvellous glimpses through arches & between narrow houses of woods & fields stretching for thousands of miles below. Moreover it has the glamour of being very near the front line. The sun was still shining as we passed it. Then Berg with a wonderful gateway, the rising sun carved boldly in stone above the gate & great coats of arms below. All this I could only just catch as we drove through. It has a moat & ramparts & all around it the fens which always give me a feeling of being at the end of the world especially on a stormy day.

We lunched with a General Lamb outside Dunkirk in a little camp of huts. He commands aeroplanes. The huts were right in the country close to a deserted château with a wild overgrown garden full of Judas trees & tulip trees & roses & very long grass. They lived in great luxury & gave us an elaborate luncheon with potent cups that went straight to my head but alas did not unlock my tongue. He told Milly that I was at first rather forbidding but that he had gathered a more favourable impression by the end of luncheon! There were a lot of people & it was rather a formal embarrassing end to the divine drive. Afterwards we motored on to Dunkirk promising to have tea with [them] on the way back. Rose whom the luncheon had reduced to a perfect lassitude had a craving to sit on the sea shore. Milly wanted to shop. We compromised & had too little time for either, & by this time there was great gale blowing & heavy clouds at sea. The *plage* at Dunkirk is the most desolate thing I have ever seen. Grey sand for miles with a few black sinister monitors & destroyers lying out at sea & rows of deserted bomb stricken casinos & hotels along the sea front. They showed me the site of their old hospital & I wondered how they could have endured it but in those days I suppose the place was swarming with life. We drove back in a thunderstorm, had tea with the airmen & dined at Cassel, rather limp & tired, with Kennedy & Hadow on the way home.

Sunday June 23rd
Duff came yesterday evening, also Alastair & Hélène (who had been in Paris). We had a dinner party as Kennedy, Hadow and a stranger, Captain Callender, came over from Cassel. I was so pleased at seeing Duff. It was a great excitement but I was anxious about his entertainment & his coming in such a crowd of people made it difficult. There was bridge after dinner & as I shared a room with Rose I couldn't sit up & talk with him. This morning I did [talk to him], snatched from the hospital.

Last night xx[8] but for the last time as I didn't like the effect.

Friday June 28th
I had a series of black depressions after Duff went on Sunday

---

8 'xx' denotes morphia

morning. He and I sat under a tree & talked all the morning—just after I made the last entry. Then after lunch he motored back to Hardelot. I felt terribly frightened for him.

On Tuesday Scally went on night duty & I was sent down to the other end of the ward (it is in fact quite a separate ward though part of the same hut) under a new Sister 'Green' & no other V.A.D to prop me up. I rather prefer to reign in my own kitchen & all this week the work has been very light as we had so few cases—one very bad complicated pneumonia, & three fractures. Tonight however a large convoy has come in & we shall be worked off our legs. <u>Note</u> I must try to be a little quicker. I have some qualms about my capacity & endurance, but they may give us more help & anyway the cases won't stay long. I shall be glad of something to do for I've felt very low all the week—at one moment I thought I must be going to have the influenza but it passed off. In desperate hope of a decent excuse to throw up the sponge & retire to bed for a day or two I quite fell into the Sutherland habit of taking my temperature every ½ hour but alas it availed nothing.

Last night (Thursday) General Ponsonby asked me to dinner in the town. I took Rose so he brought another man. We started out at six & went to see a very bad troupe who were giving the usual follies performance at the Cavalry barracks before dinner. We endured it ill enough but the dinner went off better than I anticipated. He had ordered an excellent meal—champagne, strawberries & cream etc at a funny little restaurant called Madame Bonnière in the Rue de Dunkerque. He talked gaily & by a miracle Rose & I followed him perfectly & both thought him an angel. I can't recollect anything that was said; in retrospect the conversation was what R[aymond] described as a vague brouhaha but I was unconscious of strain so it must have been all right. It was rather nice of Rose to come. I went from pure sentiment.

A book called *Trura* seems to me rather good, recommended by Maurice, turned down by Milly. I'm almost bound to like it.

Colonel Clarke brought up a drum & fife band this afternoon & played to us at tea in the field & also afterwards in the hospital. I adored the drums. They played *Quand Madelon* among other marches.

The pneumonia case has caused me some misery. The boy is very ill & being difficult to nurse & as usual the Sisters won't humour him. Hospitals are horrible places unless the nurse is a genius.

Monday July 1st

The boy with pneumonia died yesterday. It was very grim. All the time he was here he never said anything to indicate that he had one thought outside the illness & the pain, & he hated us all quite ignorantly & blindly & thought we were all against him, bullying him & hurting him. He <u>never</u> spoke of anything but the pillows & the drinks & he was very young. I never thought he would die somehow till yesterday morning. Illness must be ghastly for people like that. Everyone gets a bit like it when they are ill but we have saving moments. That death & Sister Scally's departure have depressed me terribly. Poor Sister Scally had a stroke as she came off night duty & they rushed her off to Boulogne in an ambulance that very day. We all minded it rather. She was my one friend among the sisters. I had worked so hard to earn her good opinion & support & I had really got it & I respected her nursing enormously. Now I have got to begin all over again with Green who is quite nice but not sympathetic. She is really very nice to me but I consider that she & Captain Chappell bungled the pneumonia boy. Chappell whom I liked best of the doctors at first is much the worst. Schlesinger is worth the whole lot of them.

I have worked like a black since I last wrote. On Friday night 50 new cases came in & A & B were filled up & there was no time to breathe all Saturday & Sunday. Today we have sent a good many of them away but I have about seven left, one very bad with gas gangrene. Ray the little Italian American is gone whom I rather liked. He was like a child, rather soft-hearted & boastful & naughty & exacting & ready to laugh at himself.

I hear from home that Helen looked lovely in a ballet of Barrie. Diana dressed her which was angelic of her. I had a sweet letter from her this morning. Apparently the Montague menage is in danger[9]. I have half decided to stay here until the middle of August. I somehow dread leaving this life. It seems quite empty & unreal but it's distracting. When the ward is full I get absorbed in it. I dreamt of Raymond last night. I dreamt that I lived with him without being married to him. I was so sure I was right it was very pleasant. Oh God how can I go on living like this.

---

9   Venetia Stanley married Edwin Montague in July 1915. It was not a happy marriage.

Sunday July 7th
We have been very slack since Monday. We have reduced the patients to five. I find Sister Green very easy going & our only bad case, a Welsh boy with gas gangrene, is Schlesinger's who nearly always cures his cases & is amusing to work for. A is fuller. I talk to the men there sometimes. They are extraordinarily gay & patient & pathetic. One man in B is a Yorkshireman, he talks very loudly about the war—in fact whenever he is awake he is shouting. He seemed very young & rough & on the whole pleased with life but suddenly I found a sort of fierce bitterness in him. His mother had been paralysed. He & his twin brother & one sister nursed her & adored her. The two young men did every thing for her & he told me she never had a pain or a bedsore. She wouldn't allow anyone else to touch the bed. Then the one she loved best enlisted (not my one) & when he went away she began to fret & grow iller. They knew she was dying & sent for him to come & see her. He couldn't get leave so at last he came away without it. He was quartered quite near their home in Yorkshire, but the next day the military police found him & took him away & he was put into prison in Perthshire a day's journey from Ripon & she died a week afterwards from sheer misery with his picture in front of her & he knowing it all the time, but quite helpless in his cell. He told me in a way that made me shiver. It sounds bookish & sentimental here but not as I heard it.

Today there was a comic interlude. The clergyman of 58 CCS who is a very caricature of his profession—youngish, hearty, patronising, always cheerful in a very priestly way—came down to hold a service in the ward. Green & I looked at him coldly but submitted—we both knew that the men were bored, Taffy the gas gangrene (our nicknames are very simple: he is Welsh—we also always assume he steals things) pretended to have just woken up & turned on the gramophone—his choice of tune: 'The horse the Missus dried the clothes on'.

When I had reproved him & silenced him I tried to abstract my mind from the scene & fell into a stupor. I awoke to the last phrases of the sermon it was really & truly this: **We have got to wash the face of old England clean & Jesus Christ is the soap to do it with**. This is what our army listens to on a Sunday afternoon.

Captain Bernard Freyberg VC

Oc & Beb[10] came over on Thursday. Oc should only be seen in France. The glamour his decorations & his one leg give him are tremendous here. I swelled with pride as I took him over the hospital. Beb poor dear looked rather dusty & dull. He rather annoyed me by making a peck at me on arrival, drank a whole bottle of wine so that there was none left for anyone else (Milly is rather sparing of it) & characteristically outstayed Oc who dashed off with a famous inventor of Trench mortars as soon as lunch was over, & without a qualm thrust himself on Rose for the afternoon. I shamefully behaved just like the rest of his family do & fled to the ward.

Last night (Saturday) was the queerest in some ways that I have spent here. We went to the sports of the 88th Brigade & dined with Freyberg afterwards. He was in a state of abnormal excitement all the time. He spent his one day of holiday (I afterwards discovered) in making preparations for it in Boulogne, i.e. buying food for an enormous dinner. Divisional sports are generally the sleepiest things in the world, but yesterday everyone was binged up to a pitch of keenness that quite infected one. Rose & I gasped with excitement over the races & the football. Milly came but felt ill & went back before dinner but left four of us V.A.Ds to spend the evening

---

10 The nicknames of Raymond's younger brothers, Arthur & Herbert Asquith

with the military. The dinner party consisted of us 4, Freyberg, the colonels of his brigade & the brigade staff. They all got rather drunk but not indecently so. The brigade is crazy about Freyberg. I never saw a man so worshipped or so sensitive to it. I think he is going mad. I sat next him at dinner with Colonel Clark of the Worcesters on the other side. Freyberg talked in a manner that disconcerted me more than I can say: hot abrupt whispers about life & death but always about himself. He harped hysterically on his friendship for Oc & Patrick[11] in these asides & repeated himself over & over again & the rest of the time he was forcing the note of hilarity or whipping up the tragical little festivity in a way that quite frightened me. Afterwards there was a follies show, rather good of its kind with a really funny man on bicycle, I still sitting next Freyberg who was one degree more drunk, more intense & more abrupt than at dinner. We didn't get home till one.

Tonight Hadow & Kennedy came to dinner—very restful after the 29th Division & Hadow brought me a present of a very lovely vestment which he had picked up in the trenches somewhere. I was so surprised, it was sweet of him. Tomorrow I have a morning off.

Friday 12th July
On Monday night we dined with Kennedy & Hadow at Cassel. The place was as lovely as ever—we dined on a balcony looking out over some thousands of misty miles with a stage thunderstorm going on, but the talk was unutterably tiresome, sustained mainly by Hadow & concerned solely with personalities, not that I deprecate that, only for good talk about people you must have intimacy & equality. Freyberg has come out into the open & is courting Rose in a somewhat rustic manner. He dined with us on Tuesday after the Divisional sports & to her immense amusement & I may say delight showed his hand pretty plainly. One can't be sorry for him even if he is in earnest which is doubtful, but he makes a most lamentable display. Fancy deliberately, without any weapons, any reconnaissance, any knowledge of the ground & the enemy's forces, entangling yourself with a woman who is bound to laugh at you. I should have thought that Rosemary's face would have given him a clue. But perhaps it is his

---

11   Patrick Shaw Stewart

way of enjoying himself & he is not very sensitive to the ridiculous. He wrote a letter yesterday beginning *Dear Lady Rosemary* and ending up *Bless you*.

I have heard from Diana, a sweet letter describing Breccles with a very good account in it of Montague with a tiny axe cutting down a tree so slender it had to be staked & having to rest his huge perspiring bulk after every herculean stroke. He must scare the nymphs a bit. I have taken to reading Racine. I've read *Berenice*, *Andromaque* & *Britannicus*. Of these I like *Berenice* the best and *Andromaque* the least. [One page torn out]. He seems to me to miss a great chance in *Andromaque*—a subject made to his hand too. He ought to have written it better than anyone, instead of which the play is all about Hermione, a shrew—not even a good shrew, just a stage conception of a jealous woman.

There is a great sense of disquiet & anticipation here—but it goes on so long that one gets accustomed to it. The ninth Division was going to make a small attack this week if the wind was favourable but we have heard nothing of it yet. There are a lot of rumours, everyone is expecting a big German move quite soon but no-one has an idea where it will be. On the whole they think not here because it's rather late in the summer to attack in a country that can be flooded so easily.

I have gone back to the A end of the ward, & work under sister Cornish. Batt returned from leave & as she had always been with Green in B I made room for her. I was very lucky not to be sent out of the ward altogether, but a pleading glance at matron did the trick & poor Erskine was shunted most unjustifiably. The two wards were pleased because Erskine bores them & I was much relieved. I work quite hard there but Cornish who is a silly little thing (collects silver spoons with the names of all the towns she has been in engraved on the handles) adores me & gives me a good deal of spare time. I feel ashamed of being so terribly insincere in hospital.

Saturday [sic] July 14th
Have felt rather ill for two days—& everything gets on my nerves—though really I make a great point of having no nerves, & the word which [is] cruelly abused here irritates me. Even Rosie's childish

coarseness rather bored me. She seemed aggressive & unsubtle to my subdued eyes. It's only a mood—I like so much best being appreciative. I spent my off time this afternoon—of which I cadged an unfairly large allowance by yawning in Cornish's face—in bed. A year ago last September the exit would have been lovely & honourable & not very hard. How could I condemn myself to this. I write this in bed to which restless anchorage I have hurried leaving Freyberg to pursue his courtship of Rose.

Saturday July 20th
Last night we had a great adventure. Stated baldly it amounted to this. Freyberg took me & Rose dressed as Tommies in a motor car beyond Hazebrouck to the front line. We then got out (the road in front of us was heavily shelled & we couldn't go much further), went into the outpost trenches, crawled out into No Man's Land as far as the barbed wire entanglement, returned safely home by car without a hitch. Freyberg planned the expedition with us some days before—I'm bound to say at our suggestion. Rose was half hearted about it at first, I mad keen but Freyberg the most eager of all. Rose worked on my fears a good deal. It wasn't so much the guns that frightened us as the scandal of being found out. The hospital would have been disgraced, Freyberg cashiered & Milly betrayed by me, but F's amazing energy about it & my secret persistence carried it through. I thought that probably Rose would be killed by a chance shot & then I should never hold up my head again. I didn't dare think beyond the appointed day, & yet I felt that having the chance we must go.

I grossly overestimated the danger but was quite spellbound & fatalistic about it. I pin in the plan [see following pages] that Freyberg wrote out for me. I think he would have taken me without Rosy but the pleasure of it lay for him in taking her & she would insist on coming if I went. Of course it made dressing up more fun if we went together, but her presence was the terror in it for me. We planned it originally for Saturday night but on Thursday F dashed in to say it must be a day sooner as his Brigade was moving and an attack expected. He had reconnoitred the place he meant to take us to very carefully & unless we had a stroke of ghastly luck all would be well.

For two days Rose & I blanched with terror whenever we caught each other's eyes but Freyberg was perfect about it. Yesterday evening we escaped from hospital at tea time & tried on our clothes supplied by F—all was going well, we were to leave the house at 9.30, walk down the road till we met Freyberg's runner, a Newfoundlander who was called Knee, & wait with him till Freyberg picked us up in the car. There was this complication that the driver of the car must suspect nothing. At seven came a message from the hospital to say that a big convoy was expected & would Rose if she was in come down to the theatre at once. She wavered, cried with misery, but couldn't bring herself to go so we pretended that we had already started (having already warned them that we would be out for dinner) & lay hidden in my room till the moment came to start. It, this disregarded summons, seemed to add an extra touch of wantonness & folly to our evening & Rose cried & moaned as we heard the ambulances arrive. I was more or less unaffected personally as the work in my ward didn't begin till late when the cases came back there from the theatre & I shouldn't anyhow have been wanted there at night, but I sympathised a good deal with Rose, feared Freyberg's disappointment if she didn't come & yet felt that God was giving me a way of getting her out of it if only I could take it & throw all my weight against her leaving the post of duty. Somehow I couldn't so we hardened our hearts & stuck to the plan. Once we started, looking I must confess most unlike private soldiers though Rose in the dark might have passed for a young boy, every qualm dropped from us, it was pure romance. I shall never forget walking down the road in the trysting place. There was a moon in a stainless sky. We had a slight jar at the meeting place for Knee mistook us (greatly to our credit) for the military police—he called them the MPs & I couldn't think what he meant, but soon he discovered his error & then Freyberg came up in a car sitting in front with the driver & shouted to us 'Why the bloody hell don't you be quick?' & we tumbled into the back of the car & were off. Hazebrouck looked very ghostly & beautiful & stricken in the moonlight, probably by day it isn't so good. When we got some way beyond it the shelling began but it wasn't at all alarming to me because I can't estimate distance at all. However presently Freyberg said we couldn't go on so we jumped out greatly to the driver's relief

& Freyberg & Rose & Knee & I walked down a very narrow, shallow trench. It was an outpost, some way in front of our main line & had no soldiers in it that I could see. He had brought a thermos bottle full of coffee which he gave us & some biscuits. The shelling continued along the road but it was some distance away from us by now. The sky was full of fireworks on our left but in front all was still with a very bright moon shining over an open space & then not far off a line of dark trees where we were told the German outposts would be. We crawled out into the open space which turned into a field of high waving oats in which we made a deep furrow. Presently Freyberg [said] he would only take one of us on at a time as far as the oats so he took Rose first because he wanted to kiss her & I lay hidden in the corn by myself, not frightened but very much keyed up & wondering if anything would happen. Then they came back nestling a little & I followed him as far as the wire. When we got there he kissed my hand & said 'Isn't it damned funny' & some other things which I can't remember. Our journey home was uneventful. The whole thing was much less dangerous & difficult than I expected but [had] somehow thought it childish & wrong & bad form to do it. I felt so excited & adventurous over it that I wouldn't have missed it for anything. It's the only positively happy thing that I've done for two years, Is it a betrayal of Raymond to have been happy for an hour or two? I think not for the chief alarm lay in the two facts that I just might have been killed & that I was seeing the sort of thing that he saw. I know that it is very false to see war as a romance but it is a comfort that one can do it sometimes & the loveliness of that moonlit field with guns all round it is a thing I shall never forget. Freyberg was very sweet & childish about it. I never liked him so much before. He took great care of us too. I got back with a splitting headache at 2 am.

At eight o'clock I found our ward much fuller than when I left it, mostly bad fracture cases [one word illegible]. The wounded are nearly all Scotch of the ninth Division & they got hit in making a local & successful attack at Meteren (beyond Cassel). I haven't had time to talk to them much yet but one, a very young boy, harrowed me dreadfully. It is now 11 o'clock & Rose has just come in from the operating theatre where she has been ever since two when we got home.

[The following is a transcription of four pages
of MS notes written in pencil by
Freyberg for KA, labelled Copy no 2]

Secret Special Operation order F₁
Reference Attached map F₁ 1/40000

Information
On Sat night (20th July 1918) a minor operation will be attempted by a special party.
The minor operation is to take the form of a reconnaissance of our wire in front of ANKLE FARM

Details of troops
O.C. Capt. B Freyberg
Extra Guide Pvte Knee R. Newfoundland Rgt
Lance Corpl (unpaid) Asquith
Private Leveson-Gower

Plan
The element of surprise to play a considerable part in this enterprise. Therefore secrecy is of the utmost importance. For position of (a) Assembly (b) Concentration (c) Zone of infantry operation (d) Route See attached map F₁.
The operation will be carried out under the cover of darkness. It is hoped there will be no artillery fire.

Method of Advance
(a) Approach March and Assembly
Troops are to reach assembly area under their own arrangements by 9.50 pm on 20th where they will be met by Private Knee who knows all the scheme.

(b) Advance from point of Assembly to point of Concentration

At 9.55 pm the advance will commence by car. All troops to reach point of concentration by 11.30 pm. During journey Officer Commandg will sit in front with driver. Remainder of the force will sit in rear with Private Knee who will do all talking should any be necessary. Care is to be taken to keep the driver from knowing about the scheme.

(c) <u>Advance from point of concentration to final objective</u>
At 11.30 pm the advance will continue on foot in the following order Officer Commanding Lt (unpaid) Asquith, Private Leveson-Gower, Private Knee

<u>Adv. To final Obj. Cont</u>
During final stages of the advance the party will carry RE material (duck board & sand bags). At 12 pm attaining our objective RE material will be dumped and party will crawl forward and examine the wire in "No mans Land". Same formation to be observed. During all stages of final advance should opportunity arise party will put down loads and lie down.

Should party be challenged from the rear Private Knee will do any talking that is necessary. In event of a crisis occurring Lt Asquith and Private Leveson-Gower will talk very quickly in French while I explain they are French refugees trying to reach their home in <u>Swartenbrouch.</u>

<u>The Withdrawal</u>
This is to be done as quickly and noiselessly as possible and is to commence at 12.30 pm 21st Inst. Same formation as advance order to be reversed. Return journey is to be done by car to position of assembly where car will be dismissed.

<u>Action in case of Hostile Attack</u>
At all times party will conform to the movements of their patrol leaders. All orders will be obeyed quickly and implicitly. In event of your becoming detached you will lie down and listen for a whistle signal which will be answered.

Notes
Battle order with tin helmets and box respirators are to be worn Helmets are to be worn and respirators at the alert position when leaders wear theirs in position. A good answer to any question you may be asked is "All right digger"

Acknowledge receipt of
B. Freyberg
Brig Gen
Commanding Operation

Copies to
(1) file
(2) Lt Asquith
(3) Private Leveson-Gower   17 July 1918

Friday July 26th
Nothing of any note has occurred since I last wrote. We have been very busy in the ward. The convoy which arrived on the night of the 19th poured into my ward & I haven't looked outside it all day for a week. The men belonged to the famous 19th Division & are far the nicest we have had. Most of them are bad fractures & had to be slung so are very helpless. Cornish & I got on admirably but now she has gone on night & I have a negligeable [sic] sister called Wilson whom I rather like. I had one day of fiascos when my ward vanity was humbled. In the middle of all the new work [we had] 22 hemorrhages & we had an operation in the ward in the evening & my primus wouldn't work but the others were kind. I shall live it down in time but it takes some doing. Today things seem slacker again. The patients are all better. The Daken tubes run smoothly at last & they have got used to being slung so it is easier to make their beds. America, the appendicitis case, has had his stiches out so I don't have to starve him any more. I actually dressed Freddy tonight. He is a boy with a fractured spine & double incontinence & a ghastly

bedsore. He has no teeth & is very foolish so that we laugh at him all day which he loves. I did the dressing beautifully with Porson, to my great pride, a more disgusting operation can hardly be imagined but it was a source of pride to me.

Milly came back on Tuesday so my holiday of complete irresponsibility with Rose is over. She came back in an abominable mood, full of nerves & terribly bothered about her own affairs. Her nerves lead her to abuse Rose for not marrying which always exasperates me beyond bearing. The things she says are unbelievable. Luckily I'm the only person who minds. Rose doesn't turn a hair & rather enjoys it. However Milly rather softened me this afternoon. She came into my room when I was off duty & poured out her matrimonial difficulties while I was lying on my bed trying to extract some old brandy for the ward from Bluey. She is rather pitiful & dewy about her love affairs & thinks the sort of things that a girl in a book thinks.

Yesterday Rose & I went to the lily wood for an hour's rest in the afternoon. We both fell asleep there.

Quite late in the evening Milly made us go to a concert in Colonel Laurie's mess at Blandecque. It was rather awful. The usual man with a woman's voice but a good violinist & a singer from the stage, Michaelis, whom I also thought rather good. Tonight Milly went to bed & Rose & I had a game of bridge with Batt & Fleet.

The men in the ward are perfect. They call Hadow the Chocolate Soldier. They talked about going over the parapet among each other. I asked them questions & they said It's all right, we have a lot of rum in us & each one says 'I hope I shall get blighty this time'. They call each other 'digger' generally.

I had some photographs of Trim today. Milly told me that Webb Bowen thought me lovely. I had a letter from Belloc. I really think that I have put down everything but I forgot Freyberg. He came down today again for the last time & came to say goodbye to me in the ward. He & his brigade are behind Cassel waiting to make an attack on Bailleul. I hope he isn't killed as I can't but like him. The Meteren attack was a great success so I hope his will come off too. I am afraid he thinks his laurels weigh with Rosie which is pitiful.

Milly frightened me by saying 'I thought when you first came here you took drugs but I see now it was only oversmoking'

Monday July 29th

Last night a scene which left a bad taste in my mouth till I managed to cleanse myself in the lily wood this evening. We had a dinner party, Webb Bowen, d'Immicour, General Paton & Colonel Black. D'Immicour encouraged by his General thought out a little scheme for taking Rose & me up in an aeroplane about which we were very keen. As soon as they had gone I, being rather tired of deception & not willing to embark on an intrigue with Milly in the house & also never thinking that she would put up anything but a faint protest, uncloaked it to her & then a storm burst that made me quite sick. She railed & raved: it is against the Army orders—& if she had said quietly I'm frightfully sorry but you really can't, there would have been an end of it but instead of this she completely lost all self control. Most of her tirade was delivered at Rosie who only laughed a little & kept pressing the plan. The awful part is that when Milly gets angry she begins to talk as if she was on the stage. You almost think it is a joke it is so unreal & theatrical, even her intonation becomes like that of a bad actor doing a big speech in Hamlet & yet she is almost crying all the time. She talked about 'serving her country' & our vileness & became really quite hysterical. I was so taken aback that I behaved in a way that I can never forgive myself for. Instead of shaking her or walking out of the room, the only two possible courses, I soothed her & laughed at her & finally kissed her. The whole thing was inexplicably degrading. It seemed to me in the night afterwards that there is no dignity or reality in life anywhere now. I have lost the power of being sincere, life is always finding me unprepared or a fraud, always surprised into unthinkable compliances. How I hated Milly last night for being so ghastly. I wonder if I ever seemed like that to Raymond, if all women seem like that a little to men at times. I haven't half described her violence & loss of control, but by this morning she had forgotten it or grown half ashamed of it & we passed it over lightly. Rosie's sense of proportion, better than mine, triumphed over the whole episode.

    I had a half day which began rather earlier than usual. As soon as Rose had finished with the operations & books we took the motor & some tea in a basket & went up to the lily wood. We settled down under the pine trees with heather all round & a marvellous view below & prepared to be a little peaceful & happy at last when who should stroll by but General Chichester who joined us, drank tea with us & talked to us for exactly an hour & a half by my watch. I didn't know whether to laugh or cry. I am bound to say Rose sustained the brunt of the talk. We discussed the relative strength of the German, English & French armies. We ascertained the number of men in a brigade, a division, an army corps & an army. We named all the brigadiers, divisional commanders, army corps commanders, army commanders in the British forces. We talked about the Governors of Ceylon, the natives of Waikiki, the climate of California. We even speculated about the probable duration of the war & still he sat heavily on the heather with one fat hand in a glove & one bare waving away the flies that settled on his monstrous face until Rose & I fell into a swoon & awoke to find the sun had set. Rose had to hurry back to a farewell dinner which Milly was giving to her departing secretary but I stayed on a little in the wood, wrote a short poem & then walked home. The place seemed very lovely when purged of intruders. My poem was bad enough & went as follows

> *Here in this lovely quiet wood*
> *I gather all my thoughts & needs*
> *My sad thoughts fluttering into foolish deeds*
> *Defeated hopes so wild so little wise*
> *The puzzled will which yet adores the good*
> *And fix them on your image that is gone*
> *Vanished for ever from my haunted eyes*
> *And yet not overthrown.*
> *And the pale country far below me ranged*
> *Where strange birds arch & the mists rise slowly*
> *The empty plains, the meadows ringed with doom,*
> *That piteous night is surely changed,*
> *Becomes tonight a place most holy*
> *Although it is a prison & a tomb*[12].

---

12   Later version: *Though it remain a prison & a tomb.* Compare another poem to RA called 'Blandanque wood' transcribed at the end of this diary. Evidently this wood is what KA calls the 'lily wood'

[KA later expanded it with the following lines:
O Love the earth was thine not mine
You spread the feast and bade me sup
And changed the water into wine
But now your lips are cold against the cup
But I half stranger in that golden revel
Afraid to stay yet more afraid to say thee nay
Ever thy thrall for good or evil
Outcast & waif who saw the blaze of light
And
…still unfinished]

I liked the walk back: the path, when you have dropped down out of the high wood & crossed the railway & the river, leads over the fields through very open country up to the aerodrome. Looking back the dark wood crests the high ridge behind you & on the face of the hill there is a quarry & one or two high chimneys of some deserted factory, ugly enough in the day time but in the mist & twilight rather wonderful. Then the aerodrome in the evening, with machines going out & coming in & strange lights & busy people glimpsed through the windows of the hangars & huts, & idle people strolling about in twos & threes in the dusk, is full of glamour a little. I saw one machine come down very beautifully & quietly & another rose with a fierce whirr close beside me & was lost in the sky while I was still gasping with admiration.

There are great preparations here for an offensive that is to be launched probably next month on the front[13]. We are going to retake Kimmel Hill & Bailleul. They say that Chichester scorned the idea of a peace this year. He is the Cowans of the Second army & I suppose in old Plumer's confidence. [Page torn out].

Saturday August 3rd
We dine[d] on Thursday with Major Duchet, A.P.M. of the 5th Army at a place called Ferfay beyond Thérouanne. There was the usual Follies show, this time more professional than most run by Leslie

---

13   The so-called 'Hundred Day Offensive' (8 August-11 November) that ended WW1

Henson. Ferfay is a Corps Headquarters & women uncommon there. Duchet & his friend seemed to be good natured jovial fellows. I had a good joke with Rosie afterwards about liquid paraffine. Coming home we lost the way—there was an air raid. Rose & Milly argued without stopping & Milly completely lost her self control & nearly cried & got angry with everyone. I suppose it was the air raid. I sat in the corner laughing speechlessly at them both. It was like a play one had seen so many times that it began to amuse one again, though as a matter of fact I never get quite used to the violence of older people— it always gives me a turn & seems worse in women oddly enough than in men, i.e. I feel a greater sense of superiority when I see Milly in that sort of state than say George, I wonder why.

We have cleared out the last of the McLeven convoy & now the hospital is empty. Yesterday it rained all day & I felt very depressed, but going home is a point to look forward to. I shall go home in a fortnight now. General Jeffreys came to dinner on Wednesday night. He commanded the 3rd Battalion [Grenadiers] for a week between Corry & Brooke. I talked to him about it & he said he had known Raymond. He had the reputation of being a terrible martinet & I remember their dreading his coming but after all he didn't stay with them long. I formed a fairly distinct impression of him on Wednesday night. He is the sort of man who thinks that all strikers ought to be shot & also all the members of the present government because they failed to conscript Ireland, with the exception of Lloyd George. Shooting him is too good for him & he ought to be hung on the same gallows as Asquith, Haldane & Grey. He thinks that you ought to pay farm workers 10/- a week & have an army of ten million men after the war, reducing the income tax to a shilling in the pound. He thinks that all newspapers ought to be suppressed except the one which is attacking the Govenment most violently—at the moment it is generally *The Morning Post*. He learns a good deal of that by heart. All the same he is rather a nice man & just, I should think, in his private dealings. He adored the Grenadiers. I think he was a little shocked at my being able to talk about Raymond as if it wasn't the only thing I ever wanted to do. People's points of view are so funny. The fact that Raymond had belonged to the Grenadiers made him soften a little bit to anyone bearing the hated name of Asquith

& there was I flinging a halo over the silly old regiment & trembling & thrilling over it & even tolerating him only because Raymond had been associated with it for some nine months. *Our thoughts are ours, their ends none of our own* & these thoughts ended in General Jeffreys & I conversing smoothly for half an hour or so & I am going to dine with him next week. Oh God.

Later:

I re-read Brooke—poems & memoir rather pleasant. Am getting on with Voltaire which I think is a fine book. This diary [ie Notebook] is nearly at end. Page 207 of Voltaire is rather good.

Here is some hospital gossip. There is a girl here called Kennedy, very plain with a composed manner, a bad figure & a cigarette never out of her mouth. She has driven one of the doctors quite mad with passion & she is going away of her own will because Captain Chappell loves her so much they can't stay in the same camp. She dined here in farewell the same night as Jeffreys—also a Colonel Hawke[14], a soft man, quite nice, reminding me however of Francis Maclaren[15] although he is tall & prematurely grey. He & Milly seem to me somewhat in love with each other. The theatre moon again.

Thursday August 8th

There has been a good deal of variety in the last few days. On Sunday August 4th we went to a big parading service of the 2nd Army to commemorate the beginning of the war—some doubt seemed to exist whether it was a memorial service, an intercessionary service or a thanksgiving for the blessings vouchsafed to us. We had been told that there were to be massed bands & a great number of troops present. The effect was disappointing. It took place in a big hangar in a little village beyond Cassel but it was badly arranged. The troops stood outside & the generals & their staffs & a few nurses had seats within, no spectacle at all, a small string band, & red tabs all round to the complete exclusion of fighters. Then the worst address which made me hang my head, not a glimmer of emotion anywhere. I hate the church more than ever.

---

14   In reality 'Hawes'. Millie later briefly married him
15   F McLaren MP (killed 1917) was married to Barbara Jekyll, KA's first cousin by Agnes Jekyll (née Graham). Barbara later married B Freyberg

Coming out I walked straight into Jasper & we watched the troops march past old Plumer down a little lane. He took the salute very well & looked a very freakish but somehow an impressive figure. Webb Bowen came & talked to us under a fire [?] of observation at the beginning of the service, which did him credit & that horrible old Chichester drove us home in his motor.

I was slightly ashamed of the hospital: Jackson & May looking like wild animals & matron with a fiery nose all very untidy in white caps, crumpled & low collars. On Sunday night a dinner party with music afterwards. General Ponsonby, H Graham, Michaelis were the guests & some of the hospital came up afterwards. Michaelis sang & Friedman played the violin & Captain Chappell sang a great deal at my rather unlucky request.

I am only recording facts. I have been in my saddest mood for the last week & nothing very personal has happened.

We dined at Bomy with the 19th Division on Monday. We were a little nervous about it as Chichester had warned us not to dine out or motor outside the 2nd Army area & our last experience of losing our way in the middle of the night with an air raid going on had shaken Milly a good deal. However it all turned out well. General Jeffrys was away entertaining the King & Colonel Hawes (Milly's latest flame) was in a great excitement about our coming & had made a great occasion of it. We dined at Divisional Headquarters, a rather romantic château in a romantic country. Going there we lost our way & drove over a lovely road, hardly more than a track, no hedges & great sweeps of cornfield on either side. I got my favourite coming to the end of the world feeling. I can't quite analyse it. I had it last near Berg. It is something to do with light & space & a road that winds a little but yet you must be able to see a long way ahead. You can get it oftenest in the evening but if the place gives it you in full daylight as well it is the genuine thing. This is vain. I don't know if my Bomy road would have stood the test. There was the usual Follies show after dinner, more tolerable than usual because less pretentious & the audience pathetically keen. General Jeffrys got back in the middle of the show. His staff doesn't like him much but their aversion is tempered by respect. On Tuesday there was a really awful Follies show at the Hospital combined with a garden party for the staffs of the neighbouring Hospital & the crocks & embusqué's of St Omer. Lord Tweedmouth & Colonel Glynn to dinner. I rather minded seeing Glyn because of the North Somerset. He was very hearty & snobbish, an intolerable man. Altogether a nightmare day.

The hospital is quite empty & I have no work & oddly enough not a farthing's worth of energy to read or write or walk. I am much more alive under muffy in spite of the physical languor.

Webb Bowen came to tea yesterday (Wednesday) & revived the plan of taking Rose & me up in an aeroplane. I rather like him because he is nice looking & has nice manners but I feel very self conscious when he is there because of Milly & Rosemary. I should imagine him to be very limited & I feel that they are expecting me to make him fall in love with me all the time. I've no objection to that of course & am quite incapable now of inspiring any feeling in anyone much less in a shy & busy General whom I see about once a fortnight in a crowd. The only good point in the whole matter is that he is going to take us flying which will be divine.

Today Hospital sports pronounced a great success. I ran 100 yards, was beaten in my heat by Rose; also I ran in an egg & spoon race which I practically won but didn't. Rosemary was rather tiresome & competitive the whole time, showed at her worst to my mind. All the others had better form. The tug of war was thrilling between V.A.Ds & Sisters. The Sisters were much fancied but beaten to the dust. Colonel Clarke to dinner for the last time as he is going home for a month & so he passes out of our horizon for ever.

I haven't read anything much, a good detective story called *Through the Wall* & Bridges' *Lecture on Poetry* which I rather liked. I had a letter from Duff, sweet ones from the children & my usual ones from Conrad & Bluey, not a word from Diana. Poor Aunt Alice [Horner] died which seemed to me rather sad but she must have been so sure of the Resurrection that it probably helped her to bear the pain.

News comes today of a Great Victory of the 4th Army south of Albert[16], we only heard the first bare facts but the unofficial rumours

---

16 Battle of Amiens (from 8th August ff), aka 3ième Bataille de Picardie, called by Gen. Ludendorff 'Der schwarzer Tag des deutschen Heeres,' British 4th Army under the command of Gen. Rawlinson with Australian Corps & Canadian Corps, backed up by Americans.

comforts of an English Home. In the afternoon a Band played for several hours and the Ladies under instruction were encouraged to dance together and to thoroughly amuse themselves. After dinner the records of the most popular tunes then being sung at the Music Halls in London were played by the gramophones. It was only in the dead of night so to speak, when it was presumed that most people had returned to rest that the serious work of training for Hospital duties was carried out.

This was the simple explanation of the extraordinary events that took place at Barwell Grange during the summer months of 1917.

Mrs Hoylake did not return to the Grange. She left Barwell on the following day and with her most of the young ladies took their departure.

Mr Dobson was never so surprised in his life when some days later he received a small parcel containing a Gold Watch on which was inscribed 'To Mr J. Dobson in remembrance of his courage and his untiring efforts for the safety of the Ladies of the V.A.D. School at Barwell Grange—1917'.

sight of blood. Numerous cases had occurred when the sight of blood for the first time had immediately caused fainting fits which had been difficult to overcome.

Another cause of failure was attributed by Mrs Hoylake to the fact that a large number of women were terribly distressed at the groans and sufferings of wounded men, especially during surgical operations and they were consequently unable to carry out their duties for this reason. Mrs Hoylake had therefore asked permission to start a school for V.A.D.s in England and to equip the hospital according to her ideas.

The first difficulty had been to find a site for the School and having heard from a friend that Barwell Grange had been unoccupied for many years owing to some unfounded rumours that the place was haunted, she had come to the conclusion that the Grange would meet her requirements for obvious reasons. Permission had been obtained for her to lease the house at a nominal rent, which was paid for by the Government. Mrs Hoylake then proceeded to equip her hospital school according to her ideas. Six dozen bottles of sheep's blood from various butchers' shops was one of the first things she had arranged for and these had been used for the benefit of the learners at the School. Blankets, sheets, floors, curtains and the furniture in spare rooms had been diluted with this mixture and one of the first duties of her pupils had been to not only to get accustomed to the sight of this animal blood but also to be trained in washing up and removing traces of it wherever it had been laid down. Gramophones which recorded moans and shrieks had also been placed in the spare rooms and these were turned on during the hours while the ladies were under instruction. The training of the ear to the noise of gun fire was also included in the curriculum.

In order to accustom V.A.D.s to hospital work, most of the training was carried out at night with the object of training them to work at night and to rest during the day.

Mrs Hoylake was herself rather apprehensive that the teaching at her school might be rather too strenuous for the very young girls who had undertaken to go through the course as probationers. She had been, so to say, very anxious to assimilate all the horrors of war that her pupils might in future have to undergo with all the of recent blood stains. In one room the police discovered a few bayonets which were still wet with blood stains and which were lying about on a table. All the rooms in the house were visited in turn. Some rooms were found in great disorder with sheets and blankets lying all over the floor, whilst others were the perfection of cleanliness and order. Mrs Hoylake herself was discovered peacefully sleeping in bed but in this room they discovered no less than six revolvers which had been recently discharged, the empty cases lying about the floor disclosing the fact that the revolvers had very recently been used. After a thorough search had been made throughout the whole house and all the evidence of foul play removed together with any suspicious articles such as bottles marked Poison, bottles containing chloroform and large bottles containing various unnamed fluids, the Police Inspector decided to remove Mrs Hoylake and her companions to the Police Station.

This decision instead of causing the slightest resentment, produced on the other hand nothing but merriment to the ladies concerned.

On arrival at the station Mrs Hoylake asked that she might be allowed to communicate direct with the Home Office by telephone, which request was granted and very shortly afterwards a telegram was received by the Chief Constable ordering the immediate release of Mrs Hoylake and her companions.

The whole affair came to light a few days later in a letter from the War Office to the Chief Constable of the county in which a full explanation was made concerning the circumstances of the case.

Mrs Hoylake, it appeared, was one of the principal Matrons in France, and had recently returned to England to give evidence before a commission sitting at the War Office concerning the shortage of V.A.D.s and other nurses now at the Front.

In her evidence before the commission she had laid great stress on the fact that ladies had arrived in France with hardly any previous experience of nursing and after a very short period had broken down and continually had to be sent home. From Mrs Hoylake's experience and observation the chief reason for these breakdowns were for a greater part due to nerves. A great many young ladies had failed in the various hospitals owing to their inability to face the wait very long for shortly after midnight several shots rang through the air followed by loud screams and groans. Mr Dobson, followed by his companions, rushed to the back door of the house and pulled the bell for all he was worth. The door was at once opened by a different young lady to the last time. She also was a remarkably pretty young girl. Her age might have been estimated to be about eighteen and she was dressed in a black tea gown of loose design made in heavy *Crêpe de Chine* with oriental coloured embroidery.

This girl laughingly enquired what their business was and after protesting against having been rung up at such a late hour, politely asked Mr Dobson and his companions to leave the house which unwillingly they were obliged to do. Speculation ran riot in the village as to what should be done. Every afternoon the band could be heard playing waltzes and other dance music in the dining room, and every night shots were heard, often as not followed by screams and moans of apparently dying people. All enquiries at the Grange invariably received the same answer: 'we are perfectly all right'. 'There is no occasion for alarm, and should we be in trouble we shall certainly ask Mr Dobson the policeman for his valuable assistance.'

Matters however could not remain in this condition. The whole village was thoroughly upset and matters finally came to a climax when Mr Dobson reported one evening that on looking through a window into one of the bedrooms on the ground floor, he had noticed to his horror that the sheet covering the bed was saturated with blood and that he actually saw one of the young ladies doing her utmost to remove the stains with a sponge. The story soon reached the ears of the Chief Constable of the county, who gave orders that the police were to raid the house, thoroughly search the house from top to bottom and if necessary convey the inmates to the Police Station.

A few nights later the police raid was carried out. On entering the house soon after midnight the first thing that the police encountered was one of the ladies hurrying downstairs, laughing to herself with her bare arms covered with blood up to the elbow. She was immediately arrested and taken to the library but refused to offer any explanation. On searching the rooms they found two more young ladies scrubbing the floors with soap and water apparently removing traces one night to carefully watch the grounds of the Grange. He accordingly made his way up to the house and took up his position behind a large and old cedar tree from where he could not only see most of the windows of the house, but was also enabled to hear any loud conversation that might be held in the reception rooms on the ground floor. Mr Dobson's worst suspicions were more than justified—soon after midnight he heard moans combined with excruciating yells emanating from most of the rooms on the first floor and although, as he admitted afterwards, he was completely unnerved for the time being, he did his duty like every Englishman would do under like circumstances and rang the bell of the front door. The door was opened by one of the young girls who was most neatly and prettily dressed in a summer frock made of pale yellow cotton *georgette*—and who was carrying a bucket of water in her right hand. The young lady assured Mr Dobson, while at the same time thanking him kindly for his enquiries, that his services were really in no way required and that everybody at the Grange was perfectly well and happy and the noise that he thought he heard must have been probably the result of his imagination. Mr Dobson was far from satisfied but seeing that nothing more could be done wished the lady goodnight in the most sarcastic terms he was capable of using and returned to his house in the village.

To Mr Dobson's way of thinking he felt that in some way the young lady knew considerably more than she was prepared to admit. In fact, in his position as the village constable he felt that he could not allow the matter to rest as it was. Unfortunately he had spoken to several of his friends in the 'Red Lion' of his intention of thoroughly investigating the affair and he now felt that with no plausible explanation to offer his reputation would suffer.

Mr Dobson therefore determined to enlist the help of two of his particular friends, Mr Close the local Butcher and Mr Turner the Ironmonger, and both these gentlemen having consented to offer their services, it was agreed that they should all three proceed on the following night to the grounds of the Grange and if possible clear up the whole mystery. Towards midnight the party took up their position, Mr Dobson behind the cedar tree, and Mr Close and Mr Turner in the shrubbery close to the dining room windows. They had not to

The Haunted House

BARWELL GRANGE in the County of Derbyshire and situated on the outskirts of the small village of Barwell, was one of those houses that are universally believed to be haunted. There is no doubt that there were very sinister reports circulated in the village concerning the house. The inhabitants of the village were firmly convinced that ghosts haunted the house every night, and the fact remained that the house had been unoccupied for a long period of years. It was on Easter Monday in the year 1917 that the astounding news reached the village that the Grange had been let to a Mrs Hoylake, a widowed lady with several daughters, and that she intended to take up her residence at the Grange without delay. In fact, the very next day vans containing stores of all sorts were seen making their way to the Grange. Mrs Hoylake herself, accompanied by five grown up young ladies, arrived by train very shortly afterwards and were driven to the house in various flies that had been previously arranged for from the neighbouring town.

Several days passed without any untoward events to mark the arrival of the new tenants of the Grange but the arrival of musicians and several gramophones caused considerable gossip in the village; in fact some of the older residents freely whispered to each other 'that the old gal at the Grange intended to convert the house into a popular Music Hall combined with a Hotel', but in spite of local talk there was nothing to disturb the quiet routine and serenity of the old world village. It came to the lot of Mr Dobson, the village Constable, to announce the first trouble at the Grange, which caused considerable excitement among the villagers. Mr Dobson, whether in pursuit of his duty or whether out of pure curiosity, determined

Appendix

*What follows is an account, kept by Katharine,
of an attempt to arrange a course for the training of
aspiring hospital nurses*

Yours shall be a paupery tomb
And roses shall turn black for you,
While young sad men who loved your face,
Destraught and pale and desolate
Will write a thousand epitaphs
For you then die themselves. Old age
Can never quell your youth, you cannot fade
And fall to dust, as others do. Some rare
Swift doom at last shall win your soul
For Hell's great fires that even now
Lash up impatient tongues to lick your feet—
You shall be strangled by a garland or
Die slowly of some opiate planned of kings
Or for the rage of one who loved you full
With gleaming dagger flashing to your heart—
What splendid suns will glow about your hair
With rays like gaudy tigers slinking through
The midnight of its forest. Ah what splash
Of light shall wake the south that in your eyes
Dwells passionate—What brindled shadows fling
Themselves on you as all that rush of soul
Goes panting with its victories to Hell
There through the red hot corridors it shall
Be met by armies of old ghosts that stare
With pain—sharp eyes to swoon once more for love
And rows of bitter kings who sold their crowns
For beauty like your own, and weary bards
Whose laurels, grey as ashes, hang above
Bleak eyes that once were fiery with desire,
And smouldering spirits that were mad for wine
And burnt their bodies with the wasting grape—
Then last the prince himself who waits for you
Impatient for such beauty and such woe!

towers of the town a little way below you. Rosemary & I used often to sit & read there. Today the air was very cool there. I read Pascal but couldn't fix my mind on it & yet I couldn't fall asleep so I didn't stay long. Tonight I feel very weak & rather unhappy after the temporary elation of the work.

I am a tinge annoyed with myself because I let Webb Bowen know that I was alone here, why I can't conceive & now I've got to have him to tea tomorrow. It was quite unnecessary. I don't know why I let myself in for it, an impulse bred of boredom I suppose but why I should have thought that this was going to make me less bored I can't imagine. I had Batt & Fleet to dinner last night. They are angels but Fleet is too enthusiastic. [Dr] Schlesinger is excellent. His cases do much the best.

I hope Mother won't be vexed with me for staying. I see the Guards have been in action today. The last convoy woke a spirit of revolt in me. It seems impossible that we can have let this sort of thing go on for four years, everybody acquiescing & taking it as a matter of course. I think of E[21] all the time. Thank God Raymond never got to a hospital.

Getting home on Monday is going to be rather difficult as I lost my certificate of identity & I've got no money left. I am very bad at the art of living. There's no doubt of this but why is it so complicated & yet so terribly hard not to live. Even the poor murdered soldiers die rarely & with great difficulty once they are rescued from the battlefield.

Here the diary ends.

KA wrote, on a separate sheet of paper, some time after Raymond's death in September 1916 the following poem. It could have been during her time in St Omer—the mood would fit with her state of mind in this diary—but its heightened, almost angry tone may point to a time closer to his death:

---

21   Her brother, Edward Horner

scene which has been repeated many times rather amuses me now I remember how indecent it seemed to me at first. Our sense of decency is the frailest sense of all—any kind of iteration is fatal to it. I've read the *Lettres à un Provincial* [Pascal] which I can appreciate by an effort of concentration.

Friday August 23rd
I never went away on Tuesday after all. On Sunday night a big convoy came in & we worked like blacks all Monday & still more & more arrived. On Monday I saw it was quite impossible to leave—we were shorthanded, one or two sisters on leave & the cases the worst I've ever seen—very bad head cases, fractured femurs, some people burnt by liquid fire & several cases of gas gangrene. I thought I was as hard as possible but I was appalled as the ward filled up. I promised at first to stay till Thursday but it's now Friday & I'm still here. To my unutterable surprise Milly & Rosemary pursued their original plan & departed for Paris on Tuesday at cockcrow. It seemed to me a very cynical thing to do. Their departure made very little difference but I was surprised that they should not have realised this. I don't suppose they did, more probably they failed to realise how terrible a convoy it was & how much the whole hospital was taxed. At one moment every corner was crammed. I don't mind being alone here a bit. I have been too busy to be lonely. Yesterday was the hottest day of the year—two men died in the ward & one on Monday. Gaston, the little French boy, helps us a lot. We have a German, a huge boy of eighteen. He doesn't speak much except to demand things rather imperiously, but more because he thinks we don't understand him than because of bad manners. The rest of the time he lies there white & silent. I think everbody has been sorry for him. Sister Green met the crisis splendidly. She didn't get rattled at all though she was terribly hard worked as she had both wards to run with me, Batt & Walker. I think she was glad I stayed, anyhow she is very nice to me & gives me things I like to do.

Today was cooler & we had made some evacuations. So in my off time I walked up to the field above the town & tried to sleep there but couldn't. It's a place that has a charm for me. It's planted with clover & on one side of it there is a line of willows, very grey & shimmering & it's always full of white butterflies. You see all the church to get home. Fleet's enthusiasms (we took her with us) get on my nerves & I couldn't think of anything to say to Lord Tweedmouth. Sidney & Michael were rather sweet tonight & a refreshing contrast to Freyberg who came over at tea time. I walked with him in the wood & he said all the same things to me that he had said to Rose last month & I felt too indifferent to point it out. Also I rather like him though he is a terrible bore.

I shall be half sad at going away from here. They have been so sweet to me. It has all seemed very unreal. It hitches on to nothing & even the days here seem as I look back quite unrelated to each other—but I certainly have been distracted & there were days when I worked hard & nothing actually hurt me & that gives one time to collect oneself & put a better face to the world.

I got a fit of loving French country too. It is rather like England but with an edge to it, & a bigger scale that dazzles me a little, & the touch of unfamiliarity about every house or gate or road, & the beautiful hedgeless cornfields catches me every time & the names too are like poems: Clairmarais, Estrée Blanche, Thérouanne, Ferfay & Aire sur la Lys.

Sunday August 18th
We have been fairly busy in the wards yesterday and today & there is a large convoy coming in tonight so I shall feel miserable at going. I gave a farewell teaparty to the hospital yesterday, a painful affair as I was kept in the ward till late & so could make no adequate preparations & Rosemary failed me abominably—went to bed instead of cutting bread & butter. However Fleet like an angel heaping coals of fire on my head stepped into the breach & got everything ready. I can't think how people can be so good. The conventions were observed & I depart I hope in the odour of sanctity. Anyway Schlesinger said I was born to be a nurse which pleased me at the moment quite extravagantly. He came to dinner, also Vaupelon of the French Mission & a man called Cecil Banbury. We played bridge & in the middle Banbury asked me how Edward was which almost killed me & him too poor man. We had a final typical three cornered argument about Rosemary's character—her distaste for men & Milly's responsibilities in regard to her when the guests had departed. The

A Bristol Fighter

anything so much. You get used to the wind in a few seconds & dodge it, & you feel perfectly safe & stable except when the pilot turns the machine or does odd things & then it is all the fun of White City. We looped a loop at the end which made me giddy, but it wasn't frightening for a moment. The change of proportion in the world simply stupifies one. Our machine was a Bristol Fighter, the best fighting machine that has ever been made & the pilot, a Major Johnstone who commands 20 squadron, a beautiful flyer. I could have cried when we came down. Then I sat in the motor & talked to Webb Bowen about aeroplanes (asking idiotic questions as I felt rather dazed) while Rose had her turn & then we drove home sordidly along the road. I hated its being over & felt rather childishly about the whole affair.

Today Sidney & Michael [Herbert] came over. We had seen them after the Horseshow last Monday which I forgot to record. The Horseshow was a tremendous affair at Ferfay put up by Major Duchett but when it was over & we were half dead with the heat & the Generals & the tugs of war we drove on to a place near Bruay where the Blues (now machine gunners) were stationed & dined with Lord Tweedmouth & the Herbert brothers. They were very sweet to us but I was so tired I didn't like it much & had longed all the way probably it is all a whirlwind of fury about nothing. Thank goodness Rosemary kept her head & vowed that nothing would induce her to anticipate her departure. I should have missed her terribly this week for we had a lot of people & a lot of patients. Guys Moors was as good as his word & convoys rolled in all Monday & Tuesday. Then the Queen of the Belgians came to inspect us. She seemed rather a nice person, plain but with a sort of faint, formal charm & she spoke to every patient in the hospital & gave them chocolates & cigarettes & never left anyone out or looked embarrassed or hurried & there were so many of them. It was a tedious business but she did it in the right way.

We had Hadow & General Ruthven to dinner. We were all swooning but Hadow prattled away foolishly enough. He brought me a queer book, not good, very pretentious, called *A portrait of the artist as a young man* by a new Irishman. It seemed more interesting than most books that find their way here, but it was formless & offensive with only streaks of imagination in it.

Thursday was a great day, for Webb Bowen brought off the flying stunt that we had planned for so long. I adored it. I had been fairly hard worked for the ward was pretty full but I got off at four & he took Rosemary & me in a motor to a deserted aerodrome on the Calais road. Colonel Hawes providentially turned up for the afternoon & Milly was so anxious to get rid of us that she had grudgingly consented to our going—queer after the tirades of the past. Apparently Colonel Hawes is the passion of her life at the moment & this is the key to her misery with Fitz though Fitz himself still knows nothing about it. Other people's love affairs seem to me strangely tortuous matters. Hawes is a tall sentimental man with dark eyes & no chin. I find him easier to talk to than most people here but he says foolish things about Beauty & pronounces his words rather like Francis Maclaren used to do. To return to our flying. It was the most perfect day, not much wind & floods of golden sun over the corn sheaves. The aerodrome looked very wide & empty & there our machine dropped down into it & I covered myself with sheepskins & goggles & scrambled very awkwardly into it. Then there was a great rush of air which took my breath away & in a moment we were high up & the world a patchwork quilt below & everything blue all round one. I never loved were thrilling. The Cavalry took millions of prisoners etc. I hope tomorrow will confirm it all. Milly said tonight I know what has prevented me being a really great woman—[illegible] with curiously Oh! What? Why? I see both sides of every question.

Friday August 16th
My last week here has been rather a full one. A good deal of work & a good many people about. At the end of last week the hospital was practically empty, my ward entirely so. We cleaned it out from top to bottom & then Milly & I went over to the Blandecque C.C.S & found it humming with activity but so squalid compared to ours that we tore our hair over the crime committed by the authorities in deliberately allowing their chest cases & bad wounds to lie on stretchers in tents instead of sending them down to be spoilt in our lovely wards. We had a dinner of Jasper, Webb Bowen & Guys Moors, the head of the doctors, & we drew Guys Moors away after dinner & flung our grievances at him. He seemed to be rather a weak man & promised at once to do more for us. Anyway he was wrong: if a small hospital is unpractical near the line he ought not to have taken any notice of us, but if it's right to use us at all, & I think it is, we ought not to have to cajole & bully. We were acting characteristically against out own interests for it seemed silly enough to clamour for more work just when we were all intending to go away.

I go back to London on Tuesday & Milly & Rosemary are for Paris. Diana Wyndham[17] has married Capell[18] after a good deal of vacillation on his part (a Violet!) & Rose is to join them there. We augur ill for the success of their union as the first thing that happened after they were married last week was the despatch of two telegrams from Laura[19] & Lady Rosslyn[20] urging Rose to go to Paris at once as Diana could not possibly be left alone with him. A letter followed of which the gist seemed to be that he had taken a dislike of her but

---

17 Diana Wyndham, née Lister (1893-1983), dr. of Lord Ribblesdale, sister of Laura Lister (later Lovat). After Capel's death she married again as Countess of Westmorland
18 Arthur Capel, aka 'Boy' Capel (1881-1919), lover of Coco Chanel from 1908
19 Laura Lister, later Lovat
20 Vera St. Clair-Erskine, Milly's sister-in-law

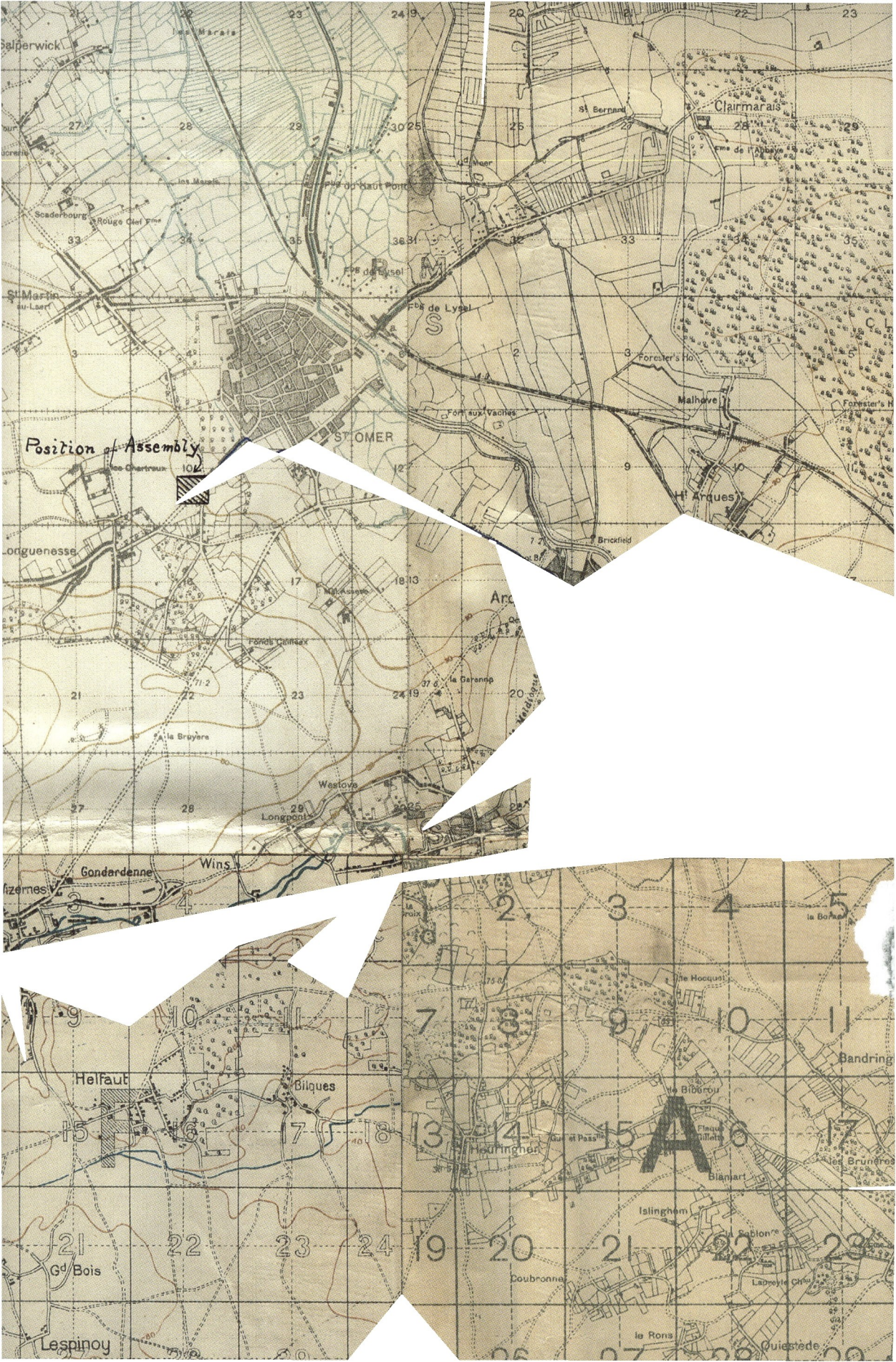